LEGITIMATE TARGET

Legitimate Target

A CRITERIA-BASED APPROACH TO TARGETED KILLING

Amos N. Guiora

OXFORD
UNIVERSITY PRESS

OXFORD
UNIVERSITY PRESS

Oxford University Press is a department of the University of Oxford. It furthers the University's objective of excellence in research, scholarship, and education by publishing worldwide.

Oxford New York
Auckland Cape Town Dar es Salaam Hong Kong Karachi Kuala Lumpur Madrid
Melbourne Mexico City Nairobi New Delhi Shanghai Taipei Toronto

With offices in
Argentina Austria Brazil Chile Czech Republic France Greece Guatemala Hungary
Italy Japan Poland Portugal Singapore South Korea Switzerland Thailand
Turkey Ukraine Vietnam

Published in the United States of America by
Oxford University Press
198 Madison Avenue, New York, NY 10016

Library of Congress Cataloging-in-Publication Data

Guiora, Amos N., 1957-
Legitimate target : a criteria-based approach to targeted killing / Amos N. Guiora.
p. cm.
Includes bibliographical references and index.
ISBN 978-0-19-996973-9 (hardback)
1. Targeted killing. 2. Targeted killing (International law) 3. Targeted killing—Moral and ethical aspects.
4. Terrorism—Prevention—Government policy. I. Title.
KZ6373.2.G85 2013
341.6′3—dc23

2012041147

Note to Readers
This publication is designed to provide accurate and authoritative information in regard to the subject matter covered. It is based upon sources believed to be accurate and reliable and is intended to be current as of the time it was written. It is sold with the understanding that the publisher is not engaged in rendering legal, accounting, or other professional services. If legal advice or other expert assistance is required, the services of a competent professional person should be sought. Also, to confirm that the information has not been affected or changed by recent developments, traditional legal research techniques should be used, including checking primary sources where appropriate.

(Based on the Declaration of Principles jointly adopted by a Committee of the American Bar Association and a Committee of Publishers and Associations.)

We are all a product of our roots and genes. While I never met my paternal grandparents, Avraham-Nathan Goldberg and Therese-Yona Goldberg, who were murdered in Auschwitz in June of 1944, there is little doubt their values and principles are an integral part of who I am today. I can comfortably say the same with respect to my maternal grandparents, Aranka Neuser and Pal Neuser, with whom I had a wonderful relationship, for which I will be forever grateful.

Contents

Preface

TARGETED KILLING IS here to stay. It is the preferred method of warfare today, tomorrow, and for the foreseeable future. However, it is not controversy free; there are legitimate legal, moral, operational, and policy concerns justifiably raised by important and thoughtful voices. To gainsay the power and import of arguments raised by policy opponents is to miss the point.

After all, the policy represents a decision by the nation-state to kill an individual suspected of involvement in terrorism. With the exception of a seminal ruling regarding the legality of targeted killing by the Israeli Supreme Court (sitting as the High Court of Justice), no judiciary has tackled the issue. In the United States, the executive branch alone determines both who is a legitimate target and when that legitimate target is a legitimate target, devoid of judicial review or legislative oversight. Given the absoluteness of executive power regarding implementation of targeted killing, the policy *must* be subject to careful scrutiny, review, and public criticism.

I write these lines from the perspective of "having been there." During the course of my 20-year career in the Judge Advocate General's Corps, Israel Defense Forces, I was involved in targeted killing decisions. This book draws on my experiences and seeks to extrapolate lessons learned relevant to current and future application of targeted killing. However, this is not a "war story" book; I seek to address broader legal, moral, and operational issues relevant to targeted killing.

My core assertion is that targeted killing must be subject to caveats, conditions, and limits. While the policy is, ultimately, predicated on aggressive articulation of the nation-state's right to engage in self-defense, that right is not unlimited. Restated: while self-defense is the basis for targeted killing, limits must be imposed on how self-defense is defined and applied. Otherwise, targeted killing will be—in simple terms—the nation-state conducting aggressive operational counterterrorism devoid of standards, criteria, and guidelines.

From the perspective of the nation-state, the benefits of targeted killing are clear: aggressive measures against identified targets with minimal, if any, risk to soldiers for the obvious reason that the killings—in the case of drone strikes—are conducted from an unmanned aerial vehicle. But while the risks to soldiers are minimal, there are other, not insignificant, risks particularly collateral damage and targeting the wrong person.

The drone strike that killed Anwar al-Awlaki has been the subject of innumerable articles, commentaries, and public discussion. No doubt, the fact that al-Awlaki was an American citizen dramatically increased public scrutiny of the policy initiated by President George W. Bush and significantly enhanced by President Barack Obama.

While I believe the al-Awlaki killing was lawful—provided reliable and credible intelligence information indicative of direct involvement in future terrorist activity had been gathered and analyzed—I am deeply troubled by the broad rationale proffered by the Obama administration for the policy. The Administration failed to articulate how al-Awlaki was connected to future terrorist activity. To that end, President Obama's Chief Counterterrorism Advisor, John O. Brennan's statements regarding the burden the administration imposes on the individual to demonstrate his civilian, noncombatant status, suggests a policy in disharmony with international law and morality alike.

The essence of targeted killing is two-fold: engaging an individual the nation-state has identified as posing an imminent danger to national security provided there is no alternative, in the name of national security, but to kill the individual. The decision must reflect rigorous application of "checks" to ensure legality and morality in the decision making process.

That approach drives this book: the recommendation that powerful checks and criteria be an integral aspect of the targeted killing policy is a direct reflection of my professional involvement in the exercise of state power. As Legal Advisor to junior and senior commanders, I gained deep respect for the impact and consequences of military force. Precisely because of my experience, I am convinced of the absolute requirement that force be subjected to checklists, guidelines, and limits. In many ways, as I repeatedly tell my students, the most important word in developing and implementing a counterterrorism strategy is "balance." Easy to say, difficult to implement, but immeasurably easier to implement when facilitated by checklists.

Active self-defense in the form of targeted killing, if properly executed, enables the state to more effectively protect itself in accordance with international law, particularly the requirement to protect innocent civilians. The difficulty in meeting this requirement is significantly compounded by terrorist organizations that regularly violate international law by using non-combatants as human shields. Nevertheless, aggressive self-defense, to meet international law requirements, must focus on specific individuals who are direct participants in terrorism and, thereby, pose a threat to society. The first step in creating an effective counterterrorism operation is analyzing the threat: the nature of the threat, who poses it, and when it is likely to be carried out. In addition, it is essential to assess the imminence of any threat; this, significantly impacts operational decision making.

To ensure both the legality and morality of drone strikes, I propose the following standards: (1) A target must have made significant steps directly contributing to a planned act of terrorism; (2) An individual cannot be a legitimate target unless intelligence action indicates involvement in future acts of terrorism; (3) Before a hit is authorized, it must be determined that the individual is still involved and has not proactively disassociated from the original plan; (4) The individual's contribution to the planned attack must extend beyond mere passive support; and (5) Verbal threats alone are insufficient to categorize an individual as a legitimate target.

Aggressive self-defense—subject to restraints in accordance with international law—reflects state action against terrorists who pose a direct threat prior to the threat materializing. There is much disagreement among legal scholars regarding the meaning and, subsequently, timing of "*planning to attack*"; nevertheless, the doctrine of active self-defense enables the state to undertake operational measures essential to protecting its innocent civilian population.

The state's decision to kill a human being, in the context of operational counterterrorism, must be predicated on an objective determination that the "target" is, indeed, a legitimate target. Otherwise, state action is illegal, immoral, and ultimately ineffective. It goes without saying that many object to the killing of a human being when less lethal alternatives are available.

Any targeted killing decision must reflect application of four distinct elements: law, policy, morality, and operational considerations. Traditional warfare pitted soldier against soldier, plane against plane, tank against tank, and warship against warship. Present and future asymmetric conflict reflects state engagement with non-state actors. In the targeted killing paradigm two questions are at the core of the decision making process: who is a legitimate target and when is the target legitimate. How both questions—in principle and practice alike—are answered determines whether the policy meets international law obligations.

The dilemma of the decision maker in the targeting paradigm is extraordinary; the time to make the decision is limited and stress filled. After all, national security is at stake. However, not all individuals suspected of posing a threat to national security are indeed a threat. A criteria-based decision-making model is necessary to ensure that the identified target is, indeed, the legitimate target. Any use of force under a self-defense paradigm must meet the following criteria: (1) The threat must be imminent; (2) The identified individual must pose an imminent threat); (3) The force used must be proportionate to the threat posed; (4) Collateral damage must be minimal; and (5) Viable alternatives to the use of deadly force are not available.

Regardless of whether a target is legitimate, if an attack fails to satisfy the requirements listed above, it will not be lawful. Thus, the Israeli Special Investigatory Commission examining the targeted killing of Salah Shehadah[1] concluded that although the targeting of Shehadah—head of Hamas's operational branch and the driving force behind many terrorist attacks—was legitimate, the extensive collateral damage caused in the attack was disproportionate.

In any targeted killing decision, three important questions must be answered: First, can the target be identified accurately and reliably? Second, does the threat the target poses justify an attack at that moment? And finally, what is the extent of the anticipated collateral damage?

To answer these questions using a criteria-based process, extensive intelligence must be gathered and thoroughly analyzed. The intelligence community receives information from three different sources: individuals who live in the terrorist's community; signal intelligence, such as intercepted phone and e-mail conversations; and open sources, including the Internet and newspapers.

In putting together an operational jigsaw puzzle, determining whether the received information justifies a response is crucial. This question is central to a criteria-based process that seeks—in real time—to institute objective standards for decision-making based on imperfect information.

To that end, the model proposed in this book for defining both the legitimate target and when a target may be legitimately engaged suggests a way forward. While inevitably subject to criticism and concern, it reflects a balancing approach

[1] Shehadah was killed in a targeted killing on July 22, 2002; as a result of the attack 14 innocent civilians were killed and a significant number injured.

required by international law in a conflict I have previously described as "mission impossible." Identifying a legitimate target in the traditional war paradigm posed minimal challenges to operational decision makers (after all, soldiers in war *look like* soldiers in war); however, defining a legitimate target in the state/non-state paradigm poses extraordinary challenges. Targeted killing is the most aggressive form of self-defense, and in the present paradigm its morality, legality, and effectiveness demand narrow definitions of how the term *legitimate target* is applied. Simply put, whether criteria-based decision making is applied determines whether the nation-state conducts itself in accordance with international law.

Writing a book of this nature is simultaneously intellectually engaging and challenging. Since my retirement from the IDF in 2005, I have written extensively on targeted killing, spoken at innumerable academic and nonacademic forums on the subject, and have been widely interviewed by the media. It is fair to state the book reflects my body of work regarding targeting killing, incorporating articles and talks I have been invited to present at many law schools, military forums, and public discussions.

Nevertheless, a book is significantly different from writing articles, giving lectures, and granting interviews—it is inordinately more complicated, complex, and demanding. Frankly, this was a challenging project for it required significant personal reflection, academic engagement, and analysis of a topic that is inherently controversial and fraught with dangers. What significantly contributed to my efforts were extraordinary research assistants.

Jacqueline Esty Morrison (S.J. Quinney College of Law, JD 2012) began working with me on the book in the summer of 2011. We created a strict timetable, requiring intensive research, writing, and editing. Jackie's contribution was enormously significant; her criticisms, comments and concerns were candid, frank, and constructive. Those were my expectations when I invited Jackie to work with me, and she more than exceeded my wildest hopes. Without a doubt, I greatly benefited from working with her.

In January 2012 Jackie suggested our tight timetable required additional help. I am sure I speak for both of us in writing that Alison Satterlee (S.J. Quinney College of Law, JD 2012) was the quintessential "right person at the right time." Alison truly represents an "all hands on deck" approach; her learning curve was sharp, quick, and most impressive. She, too, contributed enormously to the project and was a genuine pleasure to work with. Our meeting of the deadline owes much to Alison, and for that I am enormously grateful.

We worked hand in hand—as in previous books—with my then OUP editor, Kevin Pendergast; an "online," always available, editor is a model I warmly recommend; the process is enormously facilitated, the feedback is immediate, and the project is extremely focused. To Kevin, many thanks for your friendship and professionalism.

My colleagues and I at the S.J. Quinney College of Law, University of Utah, are the beneficiaries of a remarkable environment that supports and facilitates research and scholarship, fostered by my friend and colleague Dean Hiram Chodosh. For that, I am deeply indebted.

To the reader, I can all but hope that the book will be a helpful guide for a subject that demands attention, scrutiny, and criticism; and that the pages ahead contribute to an issue that is, truly, here to stay.

Amos N. Guiora
Salt Lake City, Utah
April 2012

1

AN INTRODUCTION

THE JOURNEY FOR this book began many years ago and has traveled long and winding paths. However, I feel that its time has finally arrived. I have professional experience regarding targeted killing decision-making and have written, commented, and lectured extensively on the subject worldwide. However, a book proposing a cohesive and concise framework regarding killing an individual the nation-state has identified as a legitimate target presents challenges distinct from writing articles and lecturing. I have, frankly, found the process simultaneously engaging and frustrating—typical for a book writing exercise. During the course of writing the book, my deep concern regarding U.S. drone policy significantly grew. My anxiety is not based on abstract intellectual examination of the subject. Quite the opposite: I write from the perspective of someone who has literally "been there."

Simply put: I am a proponent of targeted killing, but only when subject to rigorous criteria, standards, and guidelines. The deep-rooted advocacy of both—targeted killing and criteria-based decision-making—is largely predicated on having a "seat at the table" of operational counterterrorism for close to 20 years. I well understand the use of state power and its inherent dangers. In the same vein, I am fully aware of the terrible cost of terrorism and the extraordinary harm caused by terrorists' deliberately targeting innocent civilians. During the course of my almost 20-year career in the Israel Defense Forces (IDF), I have been involved in operational counterterrorism decision-making and seen first hand the cost borne by society from terrorism.

It is the "cost" discussion that, at some point, became the driving force behind this book. In the course of researching and, subsequently writing the book, I became increasingly aware—and agitated—of how the Obama administration was defining and implementing U.S. drone policy. The concern was both tempered and enhanced by my belief in the legality and effectiveness of targeted killing. Concern enhanced because of the ever-present possibility of collateral damage and its inevitable consequences; concern tempered because of my conviction that a successful targeted killing provides the nation-state with significant tactical and possible strategic advantages. The fine line that separates the two is just that: thin. While success is undoubtedly seductive, the ramifications of a targeted killing gone awry must give pause to decision makers. My concern is that the seemingly surgical precision of a drone attack is so powerful and alluring that it will blind us to its significant downsides.

Let me be clear: my concern is not based on compassion for terrorists. Anyone who deliberately targets innocent men, women, and children is a legitimate target. However, it is—frankly—not so simple. Application of a targeted killing structure devoid of strictly articulated and applied criteria results in significant collateral damage. While international law does not specifically quantify permitted (tolerated) collateral damage it imposes on the nation-state the obligation it be minimal. In other words, the nation-state must recognize its responsibility to proactively minimize deaths of innocent individuals. That burden is unduly impacted by the callous decision by non-state actors to deliberately place *their* innocent civilians in harm's way. Human shielding is, without doubt, both a clear violation of international law and reflects extraordinary disregard for the value of human life. As made clear during Operation Cast Lead,[1] terrorist organizations deliberately human shield *their* civilians.[2] However, that fact does not—and must not—justify targeted killing that results in undue collateral damage. Terrorist organizations violate standards of law and morality alike; that must be universally condemned. However those violations must not justify a paradigm whereby significant collateral damage is tolerated. Ethical decision-making, a moral conscience, and the rule of law must, literally, "join forces" to ensure we do not become the enemy we are fighting.[3] That statement is not meant to be dramatic; it is, arguably, the paradigm we find ourselves in today.

One of the dominant, and admittedly controversial, themes this book proposes is the state's obligation to conduct itself morally regardless of terrorists' actions and the costs they impose. I understand some will find that premise inherently immoral: fine. However, "morality in armed conflict" is a term of art (and not an oxymoron) that I take very seriously, intellectually and practically. For example, as discussed in the chapters ahead, it served as the "backbone" for an interactive

---

[1] Conflict between Israel and Hamas, December 2008–January 2009.

[2] http://www.youtube.com/watch?v=n_YP6AtdwJQ&feature=fvwrel; http://www.youtube.com/watch?v=2vHDyuSTneA, last viewed February 14, 2012.

[3] My gratitude to Margaret Hu for lucidly articulating this point.

video prepared under my command while I was serving as commander of the Israel Defense Forces School of Military Law (IDF SML). The interactive video[4] creatively addressed how soldiers are to interact with the civilian population in the context of armed conflict. The video represented a proactive effort to respond to domestic and international criticism regarding the conduct of IDF soldier's vis-à-vis the civilian Palestinian community. The criticism (some justified, some not) focused not on international law violations committed by Israeli soldiers, but rather on issues directly related to treating the civilian population with dignity and respect. The importance of the video cannot be overstated. However, the degree to which it resolves conflict and offers a road map should also *not* be exaggerated. That said, its core is essential to this book: operational counterterrorism decision-making is predicted on a complicated triangle comprising the rule of law, morality, and effectiveness.

I have repeatedly been asked whether that triangle endangers soldiers while giving the "other side" an undue advantage. Re-articulated: is my proposal not akin to signing soldiers' death sentences. That is, obviously, not a trivial question: angry soldiers and concerned audiences alike have confronted me with that question. The concern is understandable. However, the essence of armed conflict is that innocent civilians are in the immediate vicinity of combatants and there is a duty to protect them even at the risk of harm to soldiers. The burden to distinguish between combatant and civilian is at times extraordinarily complicated and poses significant operational dilemmas on soldiers; nevertheless the burden of distinction must never be viewed as mere mantra.

Distinction, then, is integral to the discussion. It is as relevant and important to the soldier standing at a checkpoint uncertain whether the person standing opposite him is a combatant or civilian as it *must be* in any targeted killing dilemma. The decision must reflect a variety of criteria and guidelines subject to morality, rational based decision- making and discretion. Otherwise, the nation-state conducts itself in the spirit of a video game where victims are not real, representing mere numbers, regardless of the degree of threat they pose.

It has, repeatedly, been brought to my attention that my proposal is antediluvian. Critics suggest the combination of modern, sleek technology and sophisticated intelligence analysis, all but ensure that Unmanned Aerial Vehicle, or drone policy, is the most effective contemporary means to conduct operational counterterrorism. The theory sounds compelling and convincing: what is more attractive than killing terrorists from the air with the use of sleek technology while minimizing risk to ground forces?

---

[4] The video was developed in full coordination and cooperation with IDF junior and senior commanders.

It is so extraordinarily seductive that how can anyone be opposed to this theory and its practical application? Someone who has "been there" should especially understand the inherent superiority of sophisticated technology and complex computer models. However, at the risk of being labeled the "last of the Mohicans," I raise my hand and say—loud and clear—not so quickly.

This intoxicating combination of technology and intelligence conjures up compelling images of silent and precise unmanned drones. All very compelling and convincing. However, important questions remain. Those queries this book addresses are intended to highlight the dangers of sleekness at the expense of decision making by seasoned commanders. There is no substitute for rigorous careful analysis predicated on a narrow definition of legitimate target taking into consideration a wide range of factors and circumstances. These must include heavily weighing ethical dilemmas and the significance of collateral damage.

We are at a crossroads: traditional state war has morphed, by force of circumstances, into conflict between states and non-state actors. Previously, international law sought to establish criteria and limits by which nation-states fought wars though violations of the laws of war inevitably occurred. Nevertheless, the rules were clearly articulated and understood, although not always implemented or respected. The era of state/non-state conflict has been marked by random attacks against innocent civilians, deemed legitimate targets, by non-state actors. The nation-state, in response, has been forced to develop and implement operational counterterrorism measures intended to protect their civilian population while striking at those responsible for the attacks. That is legitimate and necessary for the primary obligation of the nation-state is to protect its innocent civilian population, valuable national resources, and assets. Of that there is little doubt. However, the question is how the state meets that obligation: should there be limits imposed regarding the use of force? And if yes, what are those limits?

It is unfortunately easy in the face of terrorism to take an expansive view of self-defense and legitimate target. That "ease" is magnified in the immediate aftermath of an attack when the public, media, and politicians are clamoring for aggressive responses. That "call to action" imposes pressures on government and military leaders to act in order to both strike at those responsible and to deter others considering future acts of terrorism. International law obligations regarding collateral damage, alternatives, proportionality and distinction are, from the perspective of the larger public, expendable principles perceived as self-defeating, limiting state power. Former U.S. Attorney General Alberto Gonzales's disdainful description of international law as "quaint"[5] was only matched by former Vice President Richard

---

[5] http://www.legalaffairs.org/webexclusive/debateclub_gonzales0105.msp.

Cheney's referring to water-boarding as a mere "dunk in the water."[6] Both statements by senior Bush administration officials reflect an extraordinarily troubling articulation of operational counterterrorism and international law. Cheney and Gonzales suggested a paradigm predicated in which state power is subject neither to the rule of law nor morality. From the perspective of "boots on the ground," there is extraordinary danger in national decision makers imploring adoption of a paradigm best described as lawless.

That became readily apparent while writing my book, *Constitutional Limits on Coercive Interrogation.*[7] During that time I met with U.S. interrogators who repeatedly urged (beseeched is more appropriate) me to articulate that limits of interrogation be clearly defined in writing. I was struck by their deep concern that the Bush administration was creating an "ends justify the means" operational counterterrorism paradigm that would, in their opinion, inevitably result in significant violations of the rule of law. Needless to say, their concern was both justified and eerily prescient. Pictures from Abu Ghraib and confirmed reports of water boarding are but two examples of how "casual" language becomes policy and when implemented in the zone of combat, can have deeply disturbing consequences.

As discussed in this book, the Obama administration's drone policy reflects a disturbing continuum on how operational counterterrorism is conducted. My deep concern, as the pages ahead explain, is based on my experiences in operational decision-making. This book is intended to be a clarion call proposing that we undertake—immediately and intensely—a reappraisal of U.S. counterterrorism policy. The call is complicated because the circumstances are complex: the United States is a nation based on democratic values that deeply believes in ethics and values and yet, when push comes to shove, does not act in accordance with those articulated principles.

The beacon on the hill that John Winthrop articulated and that President Reagan fondly recalled[8] has, frankly, been called into question by certain U.S. counterterrorism measures. This is not the first time that American responses in the face of crisis (whether real or perceived) have reflected an "overboard" and "overbroad" approach. As history has repeatedly shown this, disturbing American tendency has resulted in significant violations of individual rights by the executive branch largely unchecked either by Congress or Judiciary. It is that largely unlimited exercise of state power that drives my deep concern with respect to U.S. operational

---

[6] http://www.msnbc.msn.com/id/15443701/ns/politics/t/snow-cheney-doesnt-support-water-boarding/#.T4w-QO1i4fM.

[7] http://www.oup.com/us/catalog/general/subject/Law/ConstitutionalLaw/?view=usa&ci=9780195340310.

[8] http://www.reagan.utexas.edu/archives/speeches/1989/011189i.htm.

counterterrorism. The manifestation, both today and tomorrow, of that unchecked use of power is the drone policy as presently implemented.

The drone policy raises profoundly important questions regarding the very nature of operational counterterrorism; how it is implemented reflects on how morality and the rule of law are applied in an inherently ambiguous and amorphous paradigm. The fog of operational counterterrorism has replaced the relative clarity of traditional war. That fog is manifested not by the state's right to engage those randomly targeting innocent civilians but the *extent* and *manner* by which the state may target and engage. It is far from sufficient to articulate an aggressive policy for the devil, truly, is in the details: what the nation-state must do is carefully define the limits of how force is to be applied. That is the essence both of morality in armed conflict and the rule of law: to deliberately operate in an open-ended paradigm with opaque definitions whereby state power is broadly defined and implemented opens the door, unnecessarily, to significant violations of morality and law.

To the point: unlimited drone warfare where limits, targets, and goals are not narrowly defined creates an operational environment whereby anyone killed—regardless whether intended or unintended—is considered a legitimate target. This expanded articulation of legitimate target premised on significant expansion of tolerable collateral damage reflects a slippery slope that inevitably results in the deaths of otherwise innocent individuals. Lost in the bluster of robotic warfare is a disturbing minimizing of the need to carefully distinguish between individuals who pose a threat and those who do not. It is important to recall that operational counterterrorism is primarily based on assessment of received intelligence information; justifying a targeted killing based on such information is sufficiently problematic. To implement a policy whereby collateral damage is not narrowly defined nor applied based on the same information that justified an otherwise lawful targeted killing, raises extraordinarily important questions of morality and legality.

Those questions have, largely, been ignored at best and unanswered at the worst. That does a profound injustice to two distinct population groups: commanders and soldiers and the general public. The former are mis-served for the very reason that Dean (then Professor) Martha Minow and I articulated in our article, "Protecting the Junior Commander"[9]: senior leadership deliberately obfuscates policy ensuring wiggle room and plausible deniability. The latter are mis-served because what is done in our collective name poses danger both to our safety and value system. Safety because of the possibility of retaliatory attacks responding to a drone attack

[9] National Objectives in the Hands of Junior Leaders: IDF Experiences in Combating Terror, co-authored with Martha Minow, in *Countering Terrorism in the 21st Century* (James J. Forest ed., Praeger Security International 2007).

that resulted in significant collateral damage; values because the policy is loosely articulated and problematically implemented.

Morality in armed conflict is not a mere mantra: it imposes significant demands on the nation-state that adheres to limits and considerations beyond killing "the other side." For better or worse, drone warfare of today will become the norm of tomorrow. If we do not have this conversation now, we will never have it. There is nothing more permanent than a temporary plan, and there are few suggestions more problematic than a directive suggestive of "do what you have to do." That was the gist of my conversations with interrogators, and that is my deep concern regarding drone warfare whose limits are not clearly articulated. There is, then, a recurring pattern that must not go unchallenged: while I support targeted killing, that support is predicated on carefully articulated limits and guidelines.

A "gloves must come off approach" has been suggested by some as essential to effective operational counterterrorism. According to this theory, given the threat terrorists pose to innocent civilians there is no alternative but to adopt aggressive measures. In that context, drone policy is effective on two distinct levels: it "takes the fight" to terrorists directly involved either in past or future attacks and serves as a powerful deterrent to those considering involvement in terrorist activity. Drone warfare is conducted using modern technology with the explicit understanding that it sophisticated, complex and lethal. Its sophistication and complexity, however, must not be viewed as a holy grail. However, because armed conflict involves the killing of individuals, the relevant questions—regardless of the sophisticated technology available to the nation state—are who, why, how, and when. Seductivity of method must not lead us to reflexively conclude, "charge ahead" for the very reason that the more sophisticated the mechanism, the more questions we must ask.

When asked my advice whether to authorize a targeted killing, I well understood the stakes; this was neither a video game nor movie. Rather, it was the most powerful decision that state agents, or perhaps anyone, can make. Ideally there is no margin for error though the reality of operational counterterrorism is that mistakes will be made. Troubling yes, problematic indeed, and deeply sobering. For those reasons, the increasing reliance on technology must give us significant pause.

My concern is not predicated on opposition to killing terrorists before they kill innocent individuals: the red flag this book raises is not based on legal or moral opposition to aggressive, pre-emptive self-defense. When necessary, predicated on a confluence of circumstances, conditions, and operational realities reflecting judicious application of self-defense principles then the state's right to preempt terrorism is fully justified. It is both moral and legal to kill a terrorist when that is the *only* recourse to prevent him/her from killing innocent individuals. However, a targeted killing policy is legal and moral only if legitimate target, direct participant, and self-defense are narrowly defined and specifically applied.

In determining whether an individual is a legitimate target, nuance and interpretation are at the core of the dilemma. The confluence between nuance and interpretation is the meeting point between morality and armed conflict. Here is the rub: while some argue killing is inherently immoral, I argue that killing in the context of narrowly defined self-defense is both legal and moral provided that the decision to authorize a targeted killing is made *only* after the threat believed to be posed by an individual is subject to rigorous analysis predicated on a narrow definition of imminence. After all, we must never forget that the essence of targeted killing is just that: the decision by the nation state to kill an individual defined as a legitimate target That is its reality. The question, however, is whether the identified individual is, truly a legitimate target and what is the basis for that decision. In order to ensure a decision-making process ensuring legality and morality, a criteria based model predicated on narrow and specific definitions must be implemented.

In other words, limits must be imposed in defining a legitimate target and when that target is legitimate. Those two definitions – -and their practical application – -are the essence of targeted killing. Broadly defining the terms is, perhaps, compelling and seductive; nevertheless that approach results in operational counterterrorism decision-making that is immoral and illegal. My involvement in operational decision making taught me one invaluable lesson: the decision to kill another human being must meet strict standards of law and morality reflecting profound understanding of and respect for the limits of state power. As discussed in the pages ahead the lure of technology is undeniable, perhaps understandable. However, that "lure" is deceptive and dangerous for it, seemingly, removes the human element from the decision making process. Nothing could be more dangerous than an over-reliance on technology that minimizes, if not negates, criteria based decision making predicated on narrow definitions. That is not to suggest that machines are making the decisions but it is intended to highlight the danger in the Obama administration's proposal that a flexible definition of imminence be adopted.

Re-articulated: the combination of sleek technology and broad definition of imminence is deeply troubling. While the former reflects significant and important advances in warfare the latter suggests a paradigm devoid of strict and narrow application of international law principles and obligations. Many, not all, would respond that the former is a positive development; the question is whether the danger inherent to the latter is fully understood and appreciated. To make it clear: regardless of the dangers posed by terrorism, the nation state cannot allow itself the "luxury" of adopting a paradigm in which "flexible" definitions of principles, otherwise intended to justifiably limit state power, are viewed favorably.

That is a dangerous road to travel, with little opportunity to backtrack. In other words, long established principles of collateral damage, proportionality, imminence, alternatives and military necessity must not be subject to the "whims of the moment" regardless of circumstances and temptation. Sleek technology presents a compelling paradigm filled with dramatic, exciting and compelling images. However, there is no alternative for pain-staking gathering and analysis of intelligence information that in conjunction with narrow application of state power facilitates implementation of criteria based decision-making model predicated on respect for the rule of law and morality in armed conflict.

Participation in numerous academic conferences, exchanges with fellow academics, and significant interaction with the media and engaged public have significantly contributed to the writing of this book. However, the book is not written from the perch of academia. While that lofty view presents certain advantages, it is not the one from which I examine targeted killing. Rather, my perspective is—literally—in the trenches communicating directly with commanders seeking my advice whether to conduct a targeted killing. In other words, "go or no go."

Deciding to go forward (or not) with a targeted killing is not an abstract decision. Thus, my analysis in the pages ahead is not predicated on a vague understanding of the consequences of operational counterterrorism. Rather, the discussion is rooted in "on the ground" reality with deep recognition of costs associated with terrorism and counterterrorism alike. The word "cost" is central to this book, for authorizing a targeted killing implies very real costs. Needless to say, *not* authorizing a targeted killing potentially implies similar costs.

Woven throughout the following discussion is a vignette that I was involved in while serving as the IDF Legal Advisor to the Gaza Strip from 1994 to 1997. Though the facts are necessarily "fudged," the vignette serves as both backdrop and introduction in the chapters ahead. The experience has served as a powerful marker for me both personally and professionally. After all, based on my legal advice, the commander would, in all likelihood, choose a particular course of action whose ramifications and repercussions would be deadly and enormous. I was the last person he consulted before deciding, and I consulted no one before rendering my legal advice. However, both the commander and I were fully prepared to make the decision based on our independent judgment, experience, skill set, and "read" of the situation.

The vignette is not intended to dramatize the setting but rather is presented as a firsthand account of the setting and circumstances in which operational counterterrorism decisions are made. We—two trained professionals—were to make a decision whether to engage, based on our decision-making skills, experience and respect for international law principles and ethical dilemmas. This is not to paint a rosy picture of our exchange: we were discussing whether or not to kill another human being. I have replayed the conversation countless times in my head; it is, in many ways, central to my professional career. Over the years, I have come to appreciate its deeper significance, extending far beyond immediate operational considerations

The issues we discussed—the possibility of collateral damage, national and international law, ethics, morality, assurance that the target identified by the source was *the* target identified by the source, the ramifications of engaging the particular individual—were all given significant weight before we reached a decision. In the chapters ahead, based on a particular vignette the following issues will be discussed: When is a target a legitimate target? How does the source know what he or she knows? Is the source to be trusted? What is the potential "blowback" from the decision? Hopefully in the end, we will see just why decision making predicted on a model that incorporates the rule of law, morality, and effectiveness, is an *absolute must* in today's world. With that, we turn our attention to the actual process and substance of targeted killing.

2

DILEMMAS, CONCERNS AND CONTEMPORARY CONFLICT

IT'S 3 A.M. Most people are sleeping or at least are trying to. Perhaps a few are having one last drink. But few ever hear the following words, and even fewer hear them at 3 a.m.: "We need to talk. The window of opportunity to neutralize the target is only open for a few minutes."

Processing such a sentence at such an hour can take a few minutes. But the voice on the phone doesn't have time or patience for niceties. From his perspective, 3 a.m. is the same as 8 a.m., or 3 p.m., or any hour of the day. The time the target can be neutralized is the only relevant time. The rest is irrelevant.

THE DILEMMA OF THE DECISION MAKER

The scenario above is not a fictional account of a targeted killing dilemma: quite the opposite. It is the beginning of a specific dilemma I was confronted with while serving as the Legal Advisor to the Gaza Strip Military Commander.[1] While the scenario, which will weave itself throughout this book, is presented in an admittedly dramatic manner, it highlights the realistic and extraordinary tensions inherent to targeted killing. There are, as discussed at length in this book, a number of individuals deeply involved in a particular targeting decision. In addition, the specific circumstances of a targeting decision are essential to determining its legality, morality, and effectiveness. That is, while targeted killing policy may be broadly articulated, each targeting dilemma must be considered exclusively on its particular and specific merits. To that end, for a targeted killing to be lawful, moral, and effective, it must be subject to a rigorous criteria-based process emphasizing rational based decision-making.

[1] I served as Israel Defense Forces Legal Advisor in the Gaza Strip from 1994–1997.

When I received the phone call described above, I was prepared with a checklist intended to maximize rational based decision-making. Though, perhaps, irritating from the caller's perspective, the list's purpose was two-fold: to ensure that the identified target was indeed legitimate and that the identified individual was, indeed, the intended target. That is, my questions sought to ascertain whether the individual identified by the intelligence community as posing an immediate threat to national security was the same individual in the commander's "scope".

The decision-making process was initiated after the intelligence community received information from a source, either human or signal or a combination of the two, regarding a particular individual. That information, according to the intelligence community indicated the individual was a legitimate target for a targeted killing. It was after receiving the intelligence community's assessment regarding the individual that the commander requested legal advice regarding possible implementation of the targeted killing policy.

In the vignette above, the decision whether to implement the policy involves a limited number of individuals: the intelligence community, a senior military commander, a group of soldiers, and a senior legal advisor. Additionally, targeted killings are also conducted either by unmanned aerial vehicles (UAVs) commonly referred to as drones, or from manned helicopters.

Regardless of *how* targeted killings are implemented, the principle is similar: the nation-state has identified a particular individual as posing a threat and has determined that there is no alternative, in the name of national security, but to kill that individual. To ensure the decision is not arbitrary and does not violate either international law principles of morality in armed conflict it must be subject to a rigorous application of criteria and standards.

I am a firm believer in the nation-state's right to engage in aggressive and preemptive self-defense subject to restraints and conditions. My support for targeted killing is premised on the understanding that the nation-state has the absolute right—and obligation—to protect its civilian population. However, that absolute right is not an unlimited right. Much of the discussion in this book will address, the requirement to balance the obligation to protect a civilian population with the responsibility to do so in a limited manner.

After all, operational counterterrorism not conducted in accordance with a balanced approach results in violations of both international law and principles of morality in armed conflict. Such violations raise significant questions regarding the effectiveness of targeted killing both in theory and practice. The challenge in the targeted killing paradigm is two-fold: to correctly identify the individual suspected of posing a threat to national security and to implement the policy in a manner reflecting respect for recognized principles of self-defense. Needless to say, articulation of this responsibility is far more complex and complicated than its actual implementation.

The dilemma of the decision maker in the targeting paradigm is extraordinary: the time to make the decision is short, limited, and stress filled. The tension is in determining whether the individual identified as posing a threat to national security is indeed *that* person. The risks in mis-identification are enormous from two distinct perspectives: killing an otherwise innocent person or not implementing the policy with respect to an individual who does, indeed, pose an immediate danger to national security. For that reason, a targeted killing decision—in spite of its extraordinary time sensitivity—must be subject to a process. The criteria-based decision-making model proposed in this book is designed to ensure that the identified target is, indeed, a legitimate target.

LEGAL AND POLICY CONCERNS OF TARGETED KILLING

Active self-defense, if properly executed, enables the state to more effectively protect itself while minimizing the loss of innocent civilians; the core principle is that the state targets *only* those individuals who are directly threatening national security. In doing so, the state is actively seeking to avoid collateral damage in accordance with international law principles that it be "minimal". "(I)n time of war or armed conflict innocents always become casualties. It is precisely because targeted killing, when carried out correctly, minimizes such casualties that it is a preferable option to bombing or large military sweeps that do far more harm to genuine noncombatants."[2] In that vein, active self-defense—subject to recognized restraints of international law principles—authorizes the state to act against individuals who present a real threat *prior* to that specific threat materializing rather than reacting to an attack that has already occurred.

There is disagreement among legal scholars as to the meaning, and subsequently, timing of "planning to attack." Re-articulated, the question is whether imminence is defined broadly or narrowly. If broadly, then legitimate target is significantly enhanced; if narrowly, then legitimate target is significantly more specific, subject to strict criteria. While the doctrine of pre-emptive self-defense enables the state to undertake operational measures intended to protect its civilian population the question is when can the nation state act. The "who" and "when" questions, then, are essential to the targeted killing paradigm; how they are answered significantly facilitates understanding how self-defense is defined and applied in the targeted killing paradigm.

---

[2] Steven R. David, *If Not Combatants, Certainly Not Civilians*, Reply to Yael Stein, http://wiki.victorybriefs.com/images/2/2e/If_Not_Combatants,_Certainly_Not_Civilans_by_Steven_David.pdf.

The criticism of targeted killing is largely based on the premise that it constitutes either extrajudicial killing or assassination, devoid of criteria defining legitimate target and direct participant in hostilities. Extrajudicial killing, according to Amnesty International, is an unlawful and deliberate killing carried out by order of a government or with its acquiescence reflecting a policy to eliminate individuals even though arrest is an option.[3] Extrajudicial killing reflects a government's policy to kill the enemies of the State not for operational or self-defense purposes, but as a means to punish opponents of the State. In examining instances of extrajudicial killings, the overwhelming trend shows that the victims are domestic political opponents by whom regimes feel threatened. Rather than arresting them, regimes prefer to eliminate them. In contrast, the targeted killing paradigm, when implemented in accordance with the rule of law, targets an individual whose arrest is operationally not possible. Furthermore, lawful targeted killing is neither punishment nor reprisal for an act committed, both illegal under international law; its primary objective is the prevention of a terrorist act intended to kill innocent civilians.

To re-state: lawful targeted killing occurs when arrest of the individual poses an extraordinary operational risk; extrajudicial killing occurs when arrest of (primarily) political opponents is clearly an operational possibility. Furthermore, extrajudicial killings are domestic in nature, and while they violate civil rights, they are not part of counterterrorism in which the state must take all measures to protect itself against terrorists whose *modus vivendi* is killing, and not political dissent. Targeted killing conducted in accordance with international law is a form of preemptive self-defense, neither punitive in intention nor implementation.

Targeted killing is also not an assassination. An assassination is the killing of a political leader or a statesman and, according to international law, involves treachery or perfidy.[4] Terrorists are not political leaders or statesmen and should never be considered as such. The difference between a terrorist and a political leader is crucial in understanding targeted killing.

A leading and vocal critic of U.S. drone policy, Professor Mary Ellen O'Connell's pointed criticism[5] has emphasized the significant collateral damage that can result from a UAV or drone attack. Professor O'Connell argues that the policy "raises serious questions under the international law governing both resort to armed force

---

[3] J. Nicholas Kendall, *Israeli Counter-Terrorism: Targeted Killings Under International Law*, 80 N.C. L. REV. 1069, 1073 (2002).

[4] Patricia Zengel, *Assassination and the Law of Armed Conflict*, 43 MERCER L. REV. 615, 632 (1992).

[5] *See, e.g.*, Mary Ellen O'Connell, *Unlawful Killing with Combat Drones: A Case Study of Pakistan, 2004–2009*, *in* SHOOTING TO KILL: THE LAW GOVERNING LETHAL FORCE IN CONTEXT (Simon Bronitt ed., forthcoming) and Mary Ellen O'Connell, *Respect the Battlefield*, CBS NEWS, Apr. 9, 2010, *available at* http://www.cbsnews.com/stories/2010/04/08/opinion/main6377556.shtml;

as well as the law governing the conduct of armed conflict."[6] Professor O'Connell is joined in her critique of U.S. policy by scholars such as Philip Alston, United Nations Special Rapporteur on Extra-Judicial, Summary, or Arbitrary Executions, and organizations such as Human Rights Watch and the American Civil Liberties Union.

While Israel's policy of targeted killings has also been highly criticized, I shall address two commentaries in particular. Professor Michael Scharf, has previously argued that while Israel can plausibly claim that its acts are permissible, it "may still be misguided, creating new legions of foes rather than diminishing them." Professor Scharf's criticism of what he calls "assassination" (a term I reject) is based on four arguments: (1) instances of collateral damage, (2) instances of mistaken identity, (3) "cascading threats to the world order," and (4) strengthening enemy morale via martyrdom. Professor Scharf does state that the war on terrorism is a "gray area in international law" and quotes former U.S. Secretary of State, Condoleezza Rice, "that it is very important that this new kind of war be fought on different battlefields." In arguing against the policy of targeted killings, Professor Scharf suggests other courses of action are possible including the "criminal approach of apprehending terrorists for trial" (referring to the Pan Am 103 case).[7]

Regarding effectiveness, Professor Edward Kaplan has been particularly insightful in arguing that an empirically based cost-benefit analysis of Israel's targeted killing highlights significant doubts from a long-term perspective.[8] In a subsequent paper, Professor Kaplan explicated the circumstances under which targeted killings would or would not be effective: (i) under certain circumstances (dependent upon the extent of backlash-induced recruitment to terror organizations on account of targeted killings, collateral killings of civilians in targeted killings, and civilian deaths caused from suicide bombings), the use of targeted killings can actually *minimize* total civilian casualties over time; and (ii) targeted killings are not employed if they are either ineffective or extremely effective at thwarting terror (since terrorists will not induce their use). Furthermore, Professor Kaplan suggests that low-level cycles of violence can occur when the government is more patient than the terrorists, but higher, stable levels of violence result when the terrorists are more patient players than the government.[9]

---

[6] *See id.*

[7] *See* Michael Scharf, *In the Cross Hairs of a Scary Idea*, THE WASHINGTON POST, Apr. 25, 2004, at B1, B4.

[8] Edward H. Kaplan et al., *What Happened to Suicide Bombings in Israel? Insights from a Terror Stock Model*, 28 STUDIES IN CONFLICT AND TERRORISM 225–235, (2005); Edward H. Kaplan et al., *Tactical Prevention of Suicide Bombings in Israel*, 36 INTERFACES 553–561 (2006).

[9] Daniel Jacobson & Edward H. Kaplan, *Suicide Bombings and Targeted Killings in (Counter-) Terror Games*, 51 JOURNAL OF CONFLICT RESOLUTION 772–792 (2007).

CONTEMPORARY CONFLICT

Traditional warfare as historically understood has, largely, gone by the wayside. Images of nation-states pitted in combat with each other have been relegated to the History Channel and the movie screen. "Band of Brothers," "Saving Private Ryan," and endless John Wayne movies have been replaced by "24," "Rules of Engagement," and "The Siege." From big battles between tanks, airplanes, warships, and a seemingly endless supply of "grunts," to conflict between a nation-state and non-state actors, modern conflict has dramatically changed.

The primary cause for this transformation is that nation-states have largely ceased engaging each other in warfare. That is not to diminish the possibility that "hot spots" threatening world order will not change constant tension to tragic war. However, for all the bellicose articulated with an occasional show of force—best described as "hold me back"—readily identifiable points of potential conflict such as India-Pakistan, North Korea-South Korea, and Israel-Iran cannot be described as reflecting "war in the offing." Rather, the current state of conflict suggests a new paradigm pitting a nation-state against a non-state actor. The former reflects the traditional world order, subject to international law conventions and treaties and domestic laws (country specific), whereas the latter is beholden solely to restraints reflecting internal considerations and conditions. Simply put, the traditional nation-state is confronted with a foe that is borderless, amorphous, and ruthless.

The difference between traditional warfare and person-specific operational counterterrorism is stark. The former is an all-out assault by two militaries armed to the teeth and hell bent on total victory. Conversely, the latter is a careful, cautious poking and probing, primarily based on intelligence gathering and analysis, seeking to identify specific individuals who pose a danger to national security.[10]

---

[10] The number of articles and the large number of SSRN downloads indicate the immense academic and public interest in this issue; for further reading on this topic please see David Kretzmer, *Targeted Killing of Suspected Terrorists: Extra-Judicial Executions or Legitimate Means of Defence?*, 16 EUR. J. INT'L. L. 171 (2005); Steven R. David, *Fatal Choices: Israel's Policy of Targeted Killings*, Mideast Security and Policy Studies No. 51, *available at* http://biu.ac.il/Besa/david.pdf; Orna Ben-Naftali & KerenMichaeli, *Justice-Ability: A Critique of the Non-Justiciability of The Israeli Policy of Targeted Killing*, 1 J. INT'L CRIMINAL JUSTICE 368 (2003), *available at* http://jicj.oxfordjournals.org/content/1/2/368.abstract; NILES MELTZER, TARGETED KILLING IN INTERNATIONAL LAW (Oxford University Press 2008); Jordan Paust, *Self-Defense Targetings of Non-State Actors and Permissibility of U.S. Use of Drones in Pakistan*,19 J. of TRANSNATIONAL LAW & POLICY 237 (2010); Afsheen John Radsan & Richard Murphy, *Due Process and Targeted Killing of Terrorists*, 31 CARDOZO L. REV. 405 (2009); Kenneth Anderson, *Targeted Killing in US Counterterrorism Strategy and Law* (A Working Paper of the Series on Counterterrorism and American Statutory Law, 2009), *available at http://papers.ssrn.com/sol3/papers.cfm?abstract_id=1415070&rec=1&srcabs=1349357*;K enneth Anderson, *Predators Over Pakistan*, 15 THE WEEKLY STANDARD 26 (2010), *available at* http://www.weeklystandard.com/articles/predators-over-pakistan; Jane Mayer, *The Predator War*, THE NEW YORKER, Oct. 19, 2009, *available at* http://www.newyorker.com/reporting/2009/10/26/091026fa_fact_mayer; Geoffrey S. Corn, *Targeting, Command Judgment, and a Proposed Quantum of Proof Component:*

Because non-state actors present dramatically different operational and strategic challenges to the nation-state; accordingly, the latter has been required to develop and implement measures distinguishable from those germane to the traditional war paradigm. Rather than facing a readily identifiable foe, the state is confronted with an individual who easily mixes into the civilian population, as non-state actors neither wear uniforms nor, generally, carry weapons openly. Furthermore, non-state actors do not hesitate to endanger their own civilian population by the use of the use of human shields[11]. The deliberate placing of non combatants in harms way by non state actors is the height of immorality; in addition, it poses extraordinary challenges to nation-state operational decision makers obligated, by international law, to distinguish between direct participants and innocent civilians.

In a nutshell, the international law requirement to distinguish between a legitimate target and an innocent civilian poses significant complexity in the nation-state/non state actor paradigm. The responsibility to distinguish between innocent civilian and legitimate target is, arguably, the most difficult burden the nation-state must face; it requires articulating both *who* is a legitimate target and *when* the legitimate target is in fact a legitimate target. These two directly related questions are the essence of operational counterterrorism—answering them requires understanding the limits of state power while simultaneously engaging in aggressive measures intended to mitigate the dangers terrorism poses.

While arguably a contradiction, the tension between limited use of force and aggressive use of force is the reality of aggressive operational counterterrorism conducted in accordance with international law. The seeming contradiction—between aggression and respect for international law principles—represents the reality of contemporary conflict. The tension is enormously magnified because of the profound difficulty in identifying (both intellectually and practically) the legitimate target.

A Fourth Amendment Lesson in Contextual Reasonableness, 77 BROOK. L. REV. 2 (forthcoming 2012), *available at* http://papers.ssrn.com/sol3/papers.cfm?abstract_id=1762894; "*Drones II*"—Kenneth Anderson Testimony Submitted to U.S. House of Representatives Committee on Oversight and Government Reform, Subcommittee on National Security and Foreign Affairs, Second Hearing on Drone Warfare, Apr. 28, 2010, *available at* http://papers.ssrn.com/sol3/papers.cfm?abstract_id=1619819&rec=1&srcabs=1561229; Harold Koh, *The Obama Administration and International Law*, Address at the Annual Meeting of the American Society of International Law (Mar. 25, 2010), *available at* http://www.state.gov/s/l/releases/remarks/139119.htm; http://www.washingtonpost.com/wp-dyn/content/article/2011/02/20/AR2011022002975.html?hpid=topnews. Robert Chesney, *Who May Be Killed? Anwar-al-Awlaki as a Case Study in the International Legal Regulation of Lethal Force*, in 13 Yearbook of Inernational Humanitarian Law 3, PIN (M.N. Schmitt et al., eds., 2010), *available at* http://papers.ssrn.com/sol3/papers.cfm?abstract_id=1754223&rec=1&sracabs=1819583&alg=1&pos=1.

11 For a discussion on the use of human shields, *see, e.g.*, Emanuel Gross, *Use of Civilians as Human Shields: What Legal and Moral Restrictions Pertain to a War Waged by a Democratic State Against Terrorism*, 16 EMORY INT'L L. REV. 445 (2002).

The legitimate target discussion is, in many ways, at the heart of determining whether operational counterterrorism is conducted in accordance with long-established international law principles. In assessing whether a particular counterterrorism measure is conducted in accordance with international law, it must be conducted in accordance with four distinct principles: (1) minimization of collateral damage; (2) proportionality; (3) military necessity; and (4) significant efforts to identify, and if operationally feasible, implement alternatives. Implementing these four principles in the targeted killing paradigm is essential to ensuring policy conducted in accordance with principles of law and morality. In addition, applying a narrow application of imminence is dependent on the nation state's resolve to respect these four principles. While targeted killing by its very nature represents an explicit use of state force, its legality is measured by implementation of these principles. Failure to consistently apply these four principles in the targeted killing paradigm directly results in arbitrary, random, and excessive use of force.[12]

The complexity of the targeted killing decision-making process is undeniable: application of international law principles demands the decision-making process be subject to narrowly applied strict criteria. Articulation, development, and implementation of criteria-based targeted killing decision making is both profoundly difficult and extraordinarily important. Difficult, because it demands narrow definition of a legitimate target, and important because it facilitates targeting (and possibly killing) an individual directly involved in a specific, future act of terrorism.

The decision to implement a lawful targeted killing/drone policy reflects a decision by the nation-state to engage in aggressive, person specific, preemptive operational counterterrorism. Development and application of this paradigm reflects an understanding that terrorist attacks are significantly dependent on the roles of specific individuals. In this vein, lawful application of targeted killing imposes on the nation-state the burden both to identify specific individuals involved in the planning and execution of future terrorist attacks and to assess that a planned attack is viable. Essential to this requirement is that the targeted individual is involved in the planning/execution of a *future* act of terrorism and killing that individual will directly contribute to protecting innocent civilians by preventing a future, specific act of terrorism.

That is, a targeted killing based on inconclusive or "sketchy" intelligence information rather than strongly indicative intelligence information would not meet a

[12] For a discussion regarding operational counterterrorism conducted in violation of international law, *see* Amos N. Guiora, Global Perspectives on Counterterrorism 180–185 (Aspen Publishers 2nd ed., 2011).

strict scrutiny test essential to lawful self-defense. Re-articulated, to ensure proportional application of the measure reflecting respect for and understanding of the requirement to apply limited use of force, a targeted killing's legality requires that available intelligence information be subjected to a criteria-based analysis.

As the chart below indicates,[13] the Obama administration has implemented targeted killing, primarily through drone strikes, far more frequently than the Bush administration. Doing so has not been free from criticism. Significant concern about the Obama administration's policy, discussed in subsequent chapters, has been raised regarding its lawfulness, morality, and effectiveness.

U.S. DRONE STRIKES IN PAKISTAN: 2001–2011

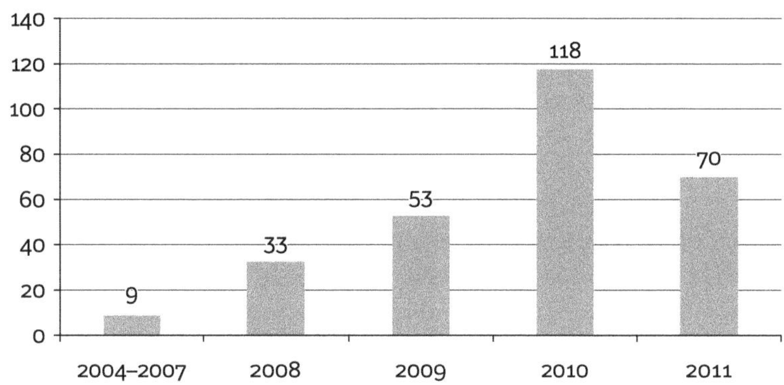

*Data courtesy of http://counterterrorism.newamerica.net/drones/2011.

NUTS AND BOLTS

In order to best understand targeted killing, regardless of one's perspective or opinion on the policy, a baseline of relevant definitions is invaluable to a rational-based discussion. That is, wherever one falls on the question whether the policy is legal, moral, and effective, terminology is important. To that end, the following

Alternatives: according to international law, the nation-state is obligated to proactively determine whether measures that cause less harm are available and operationally viable (i.e., detention rather than targeted killing).

[13] For more information on charts and graphs depicting drone strikes, please visit The Long War Journal at http://www.longwarjournal.org/pakistan-strikes.php.

Assassination: to be distinguished from targeted killing (see above). According to international law, assassination is the killing of a political leader or a statesman and involves treachery or perfidy.[14] A suspected terrorist is not a political leader or statesman and should not be considered as such.

Collateral damage: international law imposes on the nation-state the obligation to minimize harm caused to an innocent individual when engaged in armed conflict; while international law does not impose the obligation that there be no collateral damage, it similarly neither defines nor delineates what is "permissible" collateral damage.

Criteria-based decision making: in order to minimize arbitrary decisions devoid of sufficient justification, the criteria-based decision-making process imposes a literal requirement on decision makers to develop and implement a checklist approach that incorporates operational, legal, intelligence, policy, and moral considerations.

Decision maker: while circumstance dependent, decision makers include "on the ground" commanders, senior military officials, and senior government officials.

Effectiveness: in developing and implementing the targeted killing policy, decision makers must ascertain both whether the policy (in general) and its application (in particular) contribute to national security. In making this assessment, decision makers must engage in a sophisticated cost-benefit analysis seeking to balance the benefit from targeting a specific individual and the cost of a failed attack (missing the target), an attack that causes undue collateral damage, or an attack that results in *significant* retribution by supporters of the intended target (aka "blow back").

Human shielding: an act whereby innocent civilians are deliberately placed in harm's way by combatants or terrorists seeking to protect themselves from harm.[15] Human shielding is a clear violation of international law.

Innocent civilian: an individual who in no way, shape, or form is directly or indirectly involved in terrorist activities. While deliberately targeting the innocent civilian is both a blatant violation of international law and of morality in armed conflict, unintentional and minimal collateral damage (see above) is tolerated by international law.

Legitimate target: according to intelligence information, an individual who poses a direct and immediate threat to national security. The suicide bomber infrastructure effectively highlights the legitimate target discussion. (See box below.)

---

[14] Patricia Zengel, *Assassination and the Law of Armed Conflict*, 43 MERCER L. REV. 615, 632 (1992).

[15] For discussion regarding human shields, see Col. Richard Kemp, http://jcpa.org/JCPA/Templates/ShowPage.asp?DBID=1&TMID=111&LNGID=1&FID=378&PID=0&IID=3026; *Hamas Using Children as Human Shield*, http://www.youtube.com/watch?v=Jo8GqXMr3YE (last viewed June 5, 2011); *Pro Qaddafi Forces Use CNN Video Crew, Reuters Journalists as Human Shields*, http://www.businessinsider.com/pro-qaddafi-forces-use-cnn-video-crew-reuters-journalists-as-human-shields-2011-3 (last viewed June 5, 2011); *Hamas—Human Shield Confession*, http://www.youtube.com/watch?v=gowJXf2nt4Y&feature=related (last viewed June 5, 2011).

Military necessity: the measure the nation-state is considering to apply must meet the test of necessity as determined by the degree of threat posed by the potential attack it faces.

Morality: understandably a vague but nevertheless important concept whereby nation-state's operational measures, while legitimately aggressive targeted legitimate targets, must take into consideration the requirement to both treat the innocent civilian population with respect and make every effort to avoid undue suffering in the context either of a specific act or protracted conflict.[16]

Proportionality: according to international law, the nation-state is obligated to impose measures that proportionate to those it is seeking to prevent in an effort to protect its citizens.

Self-defense: in accordance with Article 53 of the U.N. Charter, the nation-state has the right to engage in self-defense. While the Article 53 restricts the right to engage in self-defense when the state has been attacked, targeted killing reflects a policy of preemptive self-defense whereby the state acts proactively rather than reactively.

Targeted Killing: a policy reflecting aggressive, preemptive self-defense whereby the nation-state targets an individual identified as posing a direct and immediate harm to national security. Its legality is dependent on an assessment indicating that the individual poses an immediate future threat rather than reflecting retaliation for a past act when intelligence information does not suggest intention to commit a future act of terrorism. Targeted killings are, in the main, conducted through UAVs (referred to as drones), manned helicopters firing missiles or "on the ground" hit teams.[17]

Terrorism: an act by an individual or individuals that targets innocent civilians for the purpose of advancing a particular cause. From the perspective of the actor (terrorist), it is irrelevant if innocent civilians are killed, injured, and/or intimidated from conducting their daily lives, or if they suffer property damage for what is important to the terrorist is that government policy is directed affected.

Terrorist: an individual involved in acts of terrorism; the actor can be involved in distinct aspects of a terrorist attack (see the suicide bomber infrastructure discussion below).

Threat: threats are either clear and immediate, or amorphous with an unclear "target" date: the former justifies aggressive operational counterterrorism, whereas the latter demands the gathering/analyzing of additional intelligence information in justifying operational measures.

---

[16] For an analysis of ethical dilemmas in operational counterterrorism, *see* Amos N. Guiora, *Teaching Morality in Armed Conflict: The Israel Defense Forces Model*, 18, JEWISH POL. STUD. REV. 3 (Spring 2006); MICHAEL WALZER, JUST AND UNJUST WARS (Basic Books, 3rd ed. 2000); Asa Kasher & Amos Yadlin, *Military Ethics of Fighting Terror: An Israeli Perspective*, 4 JOURNAL OF MILITARY ETHICS 3 (2005).

[17] For an example, see the killing of Osama bin Laden by U.S. Navy SEALS and the drone strike that killed Anwar Al-Awlaki.

definitions—relevant to the targeted killing paradigm—are offered as a means to further the discussion that follows in the pages to come:

FOOD FOR THOUGHT

In the suicide-bombing infrastructure, there are four distinct actors: the bomber, the logistician, the planner, and the financier. Determining both the legitimacy of the target for a targeted killing and when that individual is considered a legitimate target requires ascertaining the potential target's specific role in the terrorist

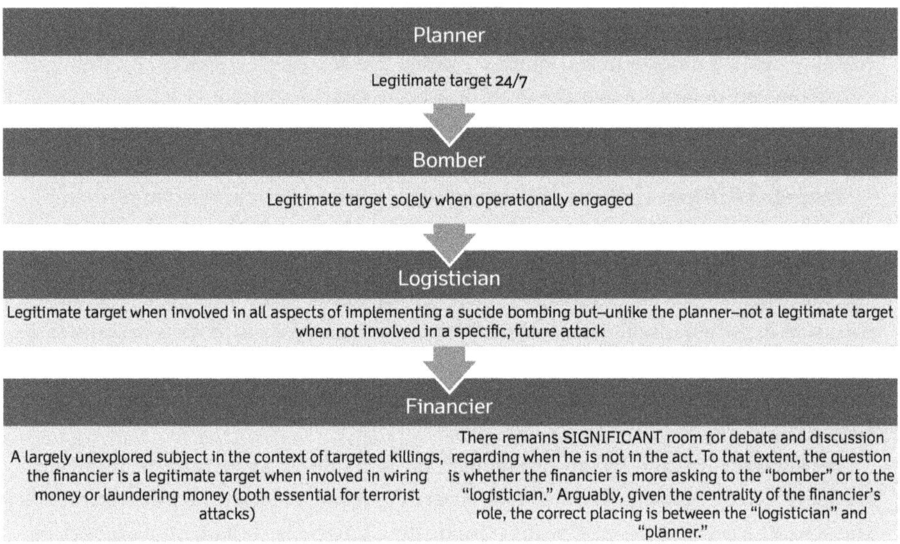

infrastructure. Both of these questions are important to subsequent discussion; to set the stage for that discussion the chart below addresses both who is a legitimate target and when that is target is legitimate.

3

INTERNATIONAL LAW

MOST PEOPLE WAKE up in the morning, get ready, go to work, return in the evening, spend leisure time with family, watch TV, and go to sleep. The pattern is repeated daily. The day is divided into neat time blocks. Cell phones have daily schedules that begin at 8 a.m. and end at 6 p.m. To "write" something in, you have to adjust the screen. Old style calendars or date books are similarly divided. There is no line available for 3 a.m. That is, the majority of us don't conduct our affairs at that time. Perhaps with a partner in bed. But that is not the sort of activity generally noted in an individual's daily logbook. Not the phone, not the calendar.

However, the caller lives on a different time clock. His life is largely sleepless, filled with nonstop activity. Perhaps he wishes he could be home in bed with his wife. Perhaps not. Perhaps he enjoys the nonstop pace of his life. The never-ending stress. The need to make decisions. The need to be needed. It could be that the responsibility is a high for him, fulfilling other needs that are too complicated to be explored. When you are in the business of constant operational tension and responsibility, who has time for self-exploration anyway? The caller's life is about the "here and now." Who has time for all that other mumbo jumbo? His is a reality where bad people need to die. "Get your ass out of bed," is what he is muttering under his breath to the lawyer on the other end of the line.

While the phone rings, 10 soldiers have positioned themselves ready for the "open fire" order. They are young men, in their late teens. Some want to be there, others not. Some enjoy the killing, the action, the thrill. Others abhor it, hoping the order never comes. Afterwards they will join in the playful banter that unites soldiers—how they would have gladly shot the son of a bitch who no doubt needed to die, and why the hell didn't the commander give them the order? Why is the commander, they may ask themselves, such a wimp? Dude, they'll say, he's all bullshit. Can talk the talk but can't walk the walk.

When the phone rings, the lawyer tells the commander to give him a minute, He's got to go downstairs or he'll wake his wife. They had made a deal years ago—he could accept this stupid position in the army just so long as she needn't know what he was doing. She didn't want to hear anything. Didn't want to be burdened with work issues—they were of no interest to her. Why would she adopt such an attitude? Because she needed to protect herself against phone calls such as this one. You want to be involved in this crazy shit? Go ahead. Just don't tell me.

The commander says to himself, "what the fuck is he talking about—give me a minute?" He has three minutes to decide whether the target will live or die tonight, and a third of that time is wasted on this wife-protecting liberal lawyer getting his ass out of bed.

Once situated, the lawyer releases the questions rapidly—Who is the target? How do you know he is the target? Who is the source? Did you talk to the source? What are the alternatives? What about collateral damage? What is the quality and training of your soldiers? What weapons do they have at their disposal? How good is their night-time vision? Who provided you this information? How do you know they don't have an agenda? This is just the start.

The commander was expecting a quick "yes" or "no." Instead he has this lawyer asking him a million questions. And every question is met with a follow-up question. Shit. What is this, "Jeopardy?" Who has time for this game of 20 questions? Why does he need a lawyer's permission to kill a fucking terrorist? Do terrorists consult with their lawyers before killing us?

COMBATANTS AND SOLDIERS

To repeat a point previously made: targeted killing is a decision by the nation-state to kill a non-state actor believed to pose a threat to the nation state. How immediate and how significant is the threat are two questions critical in determining the legality and morality of a particular targeted killing. It is for that reason that targeted killing must be guided by a rational based criteria approach predicated on a narrow definition of imminent threat. The emphasis on a targeted killing model predicated on a "narrow definition of imminent threat" is intended to highlight the dangers posed by the Obama administration's articulation of a "flexible" definition of imminence.

The two—narrow and flexible—represent opposite spectrums of a targeted killing policy; the former requires the commander to specifically focus on one particular individual, the other enables the commander to have greater leeway in defining a legitimate target. Doubtlessly, "narrow" imposes severe restrictions on commanders; doubtlessly, "flexible" increases the chances of collateral damage based on non-specific targeting. The distinctions, and their significance, are neither amorphous nor abstract; their consequences, both with respect to a particular targeted killing and the broader ramifications of such a policy have troubling consequences.

The concern with respect to adopting a flexible definition of imminence is heightened by the fact that the individual deemed a legitimate target in the targeted killing paradigm is a combatant, not a soldier. That distinction is essential to understanding the difference between traditional war and the current conflict between states and non-state actors; in the former, the legitimate target was a soldier whereas in the latter the legitimate target is not easily distinguishable from an innocent civilian. Re-articulated, distinguishing between a direct participant and non-participant imposes significant burdens on the intelligence community and commanders alike. Of that, there is little doubt. However, as difficult as that burden is, the nation state cannot allow itself the "luxury" of blurring the lines which is the practical result of implementation of a flexible definition of imminent threat.

Precisely because international law is not clear regarding the definition of a non-state actor, extraordinary care must be taken in determining when the actions of an otherwise innocent civilian pose a threat to national security. In contrast to the clarity with which international law defines a soldier, the definition of non- state actors are neither clearly articulated nor defined. In reality, the rules are initially created and subsequently self-imposed by the nation-state; conversely, non-state actors are neither beholden to nor act in accordance with rules created by nation-states and therefore act with impunity.

International law, as initially envisioned, was intended to ensure global order whereby like-minded nation-states would exercise sovereignty while respecting the rights and borders of other sovereigns. Its fundamental premise was that the nation-state (the sovereign) would exercise control over its population and border without imposing on the rights of other sovereign nations. Furthermore, international law—customary and conventions alike—established parameters for a wide range of affairs including trade, warfare, foreign relations, and diplomatic relations. International law sought to ensure a balance between two powerful competing interests: state sovereignty and the limits of state power.

As history all too readily shows, the desired balance has not always been struck. After all, war between nation-states has been a tragic reality throughout the ages. The scourge of war and its inevitable tragic suffering has served as a powerful reminder of the importance of international law. Creating order out of chaos has been essential in facilitating both ending conflict and ensuring reengagement between nation-states in war's aftermath; the framework provided by international is essential for both.

That is, then, the extraordinary contribution of international law. It is arguable that without a mutually agreed upon framework the international community, comprised of sovereign nation-states, would resemble human nature as depicted by William Golding in *The Lord of the Flies*. As Thomas Hobbes brilliantly articulated in *Leviathan*, communities are formed primarily for the purpose of protection. Re-articulated, security is more valued than unlimited freedom, unencumbered by association; mutual protection is to be favored over the Lord of the Flies.

Superimposing the Leviathan paradigm on the international community does not come without cost to sovereignty, for the reality of this model are self-imposed limits on sovereignty. However, in a world order predicated on mutual self-imposed limits the benefits—at least in theory, arguable in practice—outweigh the costs. Conventional wisdom suggests that minimizing the full reach of sovereignty ensures greater protection for the sovereign nation-state that ostensibly sharing common language and similar values with like-minded nation-states.

While wars dent that theory, history shows that international law provides the mechanism whereby nation-states that have engaged in war can "move ahead" and reestablish the preexisting world order. To that end, nation-states have created international organizations: establishment of the League of Nations and United Nations are but the clearest examples. Furthermore, SEATO, NATO, OAS, ANZUS, BENELUX, EU, and OAU are regional organizations intended to address and protect particular, specific issues relevant to their member states. Both international organizations and regional, issue-specific organizations are essential to world order, as both manifest balancing between absolute sovereignty and limited sovereignty intended to protect national self-interest. The creation of such organizations, while admittedly minimizing sovereignty, enhances national security by limiting external threats to the nation-state.

International law is the means by which nation-states create international institutions and organizations. It also provides the forum and infrastructure by which conflicts between states can be resolved. The principle that international law provides the mechanism for resolution of state conflict is essential to the targeted killing discussion precisely because a similar infrastructure does not exist with respect to state–non-state conflict. The laws of war, after all, are intended to regulate the manner in which *nation-states* conduct war; the institutionalization of the laws of war reflects the duality that war is a "reality" but also that it can and must be regulated and conducted in accordance with certain principles reflecting recognition that limits need be imposed on how nation-states engage in war.

Those limits—as articulated both in the UN Charter and in the laws of war—are intended to articulate both *when* war is legitimate and *how* it must be conducted. The effort to regulate conduct with respect to warfare reflects a twofold reality: under certain circumstances, subject to specific events, nation-states will engage in war, but there is simultaneously recognition that nation-states understand the need for external controls on how they conduct war.

In other words, what nation-states have created is a codification of war, not in order to encourage conflict, but to impose limits on how war is to be conducted. The codified laws of armed conflict as they exist today are insufficient to deal with the threats posed by modern terrorist organizations. International law is behind the curve regarding the national security dilemmas nation-states currently confront. This deficiency is particularly apparent when it comes to defining who is legitimate target and when. In order to appreciate the inadequacies of current operational paradigms, examining the evolution of targeting criteria throughout history will be particularly enlightening.[1]

THE HISTORY OF THE LAW OF WAR

In the fifth century, St. Augustine helped articulate a theory that granted moral legitimacy to warfare and became the foundation for modern military philosophy.[2] The Just War Doctrine, expanded and refined by subsequent scholars including St. Thomas Aquinas, acknowledged that resorting to war may sometimes be necessary to obtain justice and to protect peace.[3] Inherent in this theory are criteria and conditions regarding the legitimate use of force. These conditions include the exercise of discrimination and proportionality, and the prohibition against targeting non-combatants.[4]

The medieval code of chivalry, which revolved around the concept of knighthood, added another branch to the evolutionary tree of western warfare.[5] Chivalry existed as a code of conduct for knights and placed an emphasis on honor, which became a dominant theme regarding how knights could behave both on and off the battlefield. It was honorable and appropriate to target opposing knights on the battlefield, but it was against the code of chivalry to either attack another knight's horse or to attack the weak and defenseless. According to Professor Michael Waltzer, "some sense of military honor is still the creed of a professional soldier, the sociological if not the delineal descendant of the feudal knight."[6]

---

[1] This section is, admittedly, a Western-centric version of the evolution of warfare.

[2] *See* Colin B. Donovan, *What is Just War?*, http://www.ewtn.com/expert/answers/just_war.htm. For an excellent survey of the moral issues surrounding military history, *see* MICHAEL WALZER, JUST AND UNJUST WARS: A MORAL ARGUMENT WITH HISTORICAL ILLUSTRATIONS (Basic Books 4th ed. 2006).

[3] *See id.*

[4] *Id.*

[5] GARY D. SOLIS, THE LAW OF ARMED CONFLICT 5 (Cambridge University Press 2010).

[6] WALZER, *supra* note *, at 34.

The US Army specifically instructs its soldiers to "conduct hostilities with regard for the principles of humanity and chivalry."[7]

The Treaty of Westphalia (1648) established the modern framework for warfare—a framework inextricably linked to the concept of the modern nation-state.[8] Perhaps the most important development that came from this time period, as it relates to current targeting issues, was the evolution of war into a public, state-sponsored enterprise.[9] Uniforms became standardized and soldiers became increasingly professionally trained. The transition of war into a public enterprise increased transparency regarding norms and expectations of behavior and conduct.

The centuries that followed saw the codification of the modern rules of warfare. In 1863, in the midst of the American Civil War, Francis Lieber drafted the Instructions for the Government of Armies of the United States in the Field, subsequently known as the Lieber Code. According to Article 22 of the Lieber Code:

> Public war is a state of armed hostility between sovereign nations or governments. It is a law and requisite of civilized existence that men live in political, continuous societies, forming organized units, called states or nations, whose constituents bear, enjoy, and suffer, advance and retrograde together, in peace and in war.[10]

The Lieber Code specifically draws distinction among enemies between combatants and non-combatants[11] and articulates a class of protected persons and property.[12] Though never used expressly as a code of conduct by other states, the Lieber Code informed many international treaties and conventions of the 19th and 20th centuries.[13]

According to the 1868 St. Petersburg Declaration, the only legitimate object states should endeavor to accomplish during war is to weaken the military force of the enemy. The declaration's limitation on the use of exploding projectiles

---

[7] LAW OF WAR HANDBOOK 2 (Keith E. Puls ed. 2005).

[8] *See* Christopher Harding & C. L Lim, *The Significance of Westphalia: An Archaeology of the International Legal Order*, *in* RENEGOTIATING WESTPHALIA 6 (Christopher Harding & C. L. Lim eds., MartinusNijhoff Publishers 1999).

[9] *See* Alejandro LoriteAscorihuela, *Humanitarian Law and Human Rights Law: The Politics of Distinction*, 19 MICH. ST. J. INT'L L. 299, 325–327 (2011) (discussing privileged and unprivileged agents of war and the idea that fighting on behalf of a state is a public, rather than private, enterprise).

[10] The Lieber Code of 1863, http://www.civilwarhome.com/liebercode.htm.

[11] *Id.* at art. 155 (Interestingly, the Lieber Code also differentiates between citizens who sympathize and citizens who aid the rebel movement. The code goes on to say that the disloyal citizens should expelled, imprisoned, or fined if they refuse to declare loyalty to the legitimate government.)

[12] *Id.* at art. 35, 44.

[13] *See, e.g.*, LAW OF WAR HANDBOOK, *supra* note *.

attempted to ensure that weapons used would reduce the number of soldiers fighting the war while preventing unnecessary and prolonged injury, pain, and suffering among combatants.

The Hague Conventions of 1899 and 1907 established important restrictions regarding battlefield conduct which are still in effect today. The Hague Conventions are generally referred to as the "means and methods" of warfare.[14] To be defined a combatant—or belligerent, in Hague parlance—a soldier, militia member, or volunteer must meet four conditions: 1) operate under the command of a superior officer; 2) wear a fixed, distinctive emblem that is recognizable at a distance; 3) carry arms openly; and 4) behave in accordance with the laws and customs of war.[15] The Hague rules prohibit attacking undefended towns, village, habitations or buildings, and also prohibit killing or wounding "treacherously individuals belonging to the hostile nation or army."[16]

In the wake of World War II, the Geneva Conventions further codified and solidified the rules of modern warfare. Under the Geneva Conventions, armed conflicts became divided into two categories: cases of armed conflict between two or more states (also known as an international armed conflict or IAC)[17] and cases of armed conflict not of an international nature occurring within the territory of a state (also known as a non-international armed conflict or NIAC.)[18] According to the Geneva Conventions "[p]ersons taking no active part in the hostilities, including members of armed forces who have laid down their arms and those placed *hors de combat* by sickness, wounds, detention, or any other cause, shall in all circumstances be treated humanely . . ."[19] Thus, a soldier who has put down his/her weapon, has stepped out of uniform, and has returned to civilian life can no longer be considered a legitimate target.[20] Conversely, a soldier during wartime—who is in uniform and carrying arms—may be considered a legitimate target.[21]

The Geneva Conventions were drafted in the aftermath of World War II. The Conventions directly address the protection of the civilian population by clearly defining rights and obligations of both combatants and civilians. According to Article 43 of the First Protocol Additional to the Geneva Conventions, "members

---

[14] *See id.*

[15] The Hague Convention Respecting the Laws and Customs of War on Land, Annex to the Convention art. 1, October 18, 1907, *available at* http://www.icrc.org/ihl.nsf/FULL/195?OpenDocument.

[16] *Id.* at art.23, 25.

[17] Geneva Convention Relative to the Treatment of Prisoners of War art.2, Aug. 12, 1949, 6 U.S.T. 3316, 75 U.N.T.S. 135.

[18] *Id.* art.3.

[19] *Id.*

[20] *See* Law of War Handbook, *supra*.

[21] *Id.*

of the armed forces of a Party to a conflict are combatants," suggesting they have the right to participate directly in hostilities.[22] Article 44 stipulates:

> Article 44
>
> 1. Any combatant, as defined in Article 43, who falls into the power of an adverse Party shall be a prisoner of war
> 2. While all combatants are obliged to comply with the rules of international law applicable in armed conflict, violations of these rules shall not deprive a combatant of his right to be a combatant or, if he falls into the power of an adverse Party, or his right to be a prisoner of war, except as provided in paragraphs 3 and 4
> 3. In order to promote the protection of the civilian population from the effects of hostilities, combatants are obliged to distinguish themselves from the civilian population while they are engaged in an attack or in a military operation preparatory to an attack. Recognizing, however, that there are situations in armed conflicts where, owing to the nature of the hostilities an armed combatant cannot so distinguish himself, he shall retain his status as a combatant, provided that, in such situations, he carries his arms openly:
>   a. During each military engagement, and
>   b. During such time as he is visible to the adversary while he is engaged in a military deployment preceding the launching of an attack in which he is to participate.
> 4. A combatant who falls into the power of an adverse Party while failing to meet the requirements set forth in the second sentence of paragraph 2 shall forfeit his right to be a prisoner of war, but he shall, nevertheless, be given protections equivalent to those accorded to prisoners of war by the Third Convention and by this Protocol. This protection includes protections equivalent to those accorded to prisoners of war by the Third Convention in the case where such a person is tried and punished for any offenses he has committed.[23]

In 1956, the Department of the Army Field Manual 27-10 (FM 27-10) was published. It was subsequently updated in 2005 as the Law of War Handbook. FM 27-10 does not preclude attacks on individual soldiers of the enemy—whether in the zone of hostilities or elsewhere—but [24] it does prohibit specific targeting of

---

[22] Protocol Additional to the Geneva Conventions of August 12, 1949, and relating to the Protection of Victims of International Armed Conflicts (Protocol 1), 1125 U.N.T.S. 135.

[23] *Id.*

[24] FIELD MANUAL 27–100, *supra.*

civilians.[25] According to FM 27–10, combatants, and those objects that make an effective contribution to military action, are targetable.[26]

Finally and importantly, the Additional Protocols to the Geneva Conventions (1978) introduced the concept of direct participation—a new class of combatants (occasionally referred to as DPH or DPH-ing.)[27] Article 13(3) of Additional Protocol II asserts, "Civilians shall enjoy the protection afforded by [this portion of the protocol], unless and for such time as they take direct part in hostilities."[28] Civilians who take direct part in hostilities are not lawful belligerents under the Geneva Conventions, nor are they afforded the protections laid out in the various international treaties governing armed conflict.

The nature of armed conflict has changed dramatically in the past century, most notably in two ways: weaponry has significantly evolved, and the actors are quite different. The rise of non-state actors, acting outside the purview of the nation-state, has led to what scholars' term "asymmetric warfare."[29] Those who do not abide by international conventions and treaties, or the general laws of warfare, place the nation-state in an extraordinary quandary regarding the appropriate targeting paradigm.

SELF-DEFENSE

Article 2(4) of the U.N. Charter states "all Members shall refrain in their international relations from the threat or use of force against the territorial integrity or political independence of any state, or in any manner inconsistent with the Purposes of the United Nations."[30] This article expresses one of the primary tenets of international law: *prevention* of war between member states. Nevertheless, Article 51 states:

> Nothing in the present Charter shall impair the inherent right of individual or collective self-defense if an armed attack occurs against a Member of the United Nations, until the Security Council has taken measures necessary to maintain international peace and security. Measures shall be taken by Members in the exercise of this right of self-defense shall be immediately

---

[25] *Id.* at art. 25.

[26] As long as the attack meets the requirements of necessity, proportionality, humanity, and discrimination.

[27] Additional Protocol II art.13(3), June 8, 1977, *available at* http://www.icrc.org/ihl.nsf/FULL/475.

[28] *Id.*

[29] *See* Charles J. Dunlap, Jr., *Preliminary Observations: Asymmetrical Warfare and the Western Mindset*, *in* CHALLENGING THE UNITED STATES SYMMETRICALLY AND ASYMMETRICALLY: CAN AMERICA BE DEFEATED? (Lloyd J. Matthews ed., 1998).

[30] U.N. Charter art. 2.

> reported to the Security Council and shall not in any way affect the authority and responsibility of the Security Council under the present Charter to take at any time such action as it deems necessary in order to maintain or restore international peace and security.[31]

Determining the extent of self-defense is critical to a discussion examining the relationship between international law and counterterrorism. Unlike traditional warfare where militaries face off with planes, tanks, and warships, counterterrorism is characterized by an unseen enemy: battles take place in "back alleys with dark shadows." Self-defense in this environment is enormously complicated. The decision to preemptively attack a highly elusive target, oftentimes in close proximity to civilians, is based on intelligence information. The veracity of the intelligence information is central to the success or failure of any counterterrorism initiative. Operational decisions are predicated on intelligence gleaned from sources, and it is that information that states use as the basis for attacking terrorists and their infrastructure.

In 1837, U.S. Secretary of State Daniel Webster articulated a definition of self-defense, which evolved into customary international law. Webster's definition followed what has come to be known as the *Caroline* incident. The *Caroline* was a U.S. steamboat attempting to transport supplies to Canadian insurgents. A British force interrupted the *Caroline*'s voyage, shot at it, set it on fire, and let it wash over Niagara Falls. Webster said that Britain's act did not qualify as self-defense because self-defense is only justified "if the necessity of that self-defense is instant, overwhelming, and leaving no choice of means, and no moment for deliberation."

According to Webster, Britain could have dealt with the *Caroline* in a more diplomatic matter. He limited the right to self-defense to situations where there is a real threat, where the response is essential and proportional, and all peaceful means of resolving the dispute have been exhausted. The concept known as the *Caroline* doctrine was considered customary international law until a competing definition of self-defense arose in Article 51 of the U.N. Charter, which authorizes self-defense in response to an armed attack.

When can preemptive action be taken? Preemptive action first requires that intelligence information be reliable and corroborated. Furthermore, for preemptive action to be legitimate, it must be proportional in the context of the attack it seeks to prevent. In determining proportionality, decision makers must take into consideration both the immediacy of the threat and its potential severity.

---

[31] U.N. Charter art. 51.

The intent of Article 51 was to limit the invocation of the right to self-defense. Any limitation, however, required a discussion regarding the right to engage in anticipatory self-defense. States need to not only defend themselves against ongoing attacks, but also to act preemptively to prevent aggressive acts from being carried out. Customary international law permits a state to respond to a threat and infringe on the territorial sovereignty of another nation when four criteria are met: (1) it is acting in self-defense; (2) the attack is substantial and military (i.e., not an "isolated armed incident"); (3) the offending nation is complicit, unwilling, or unable to prevent further attacks; (4) the attack is widespread and imminent.[32]

The development of a new body of international law providing legal justification for such actions (active self-defense against a non-state actor) must be consistent with existing principles on obligations including proportionality, military necessity, collateral damage, and exhaustion or unavailability of peaceful alternative.

In undertaking operational counterterrorism, decision makers are increasingly faced with the following dilemma: whether an action—be it preventative or responsive—can be undertaken in the event it involves violating the sovereignty of another nation-state. In conjunction with self-defense, the question of failed states providing material support to terrorism must be addressed in the context of international law. When the United States attacked al Qaeda and the Taliban in Afghanistan following 9/11, the United States was attacking a sovereign nation. It was argued that Afghanistan was not strong enough to try to control or limit terrorists within their borders; therefore, other nations affected by those terrorists could take action. The United States warned the Taliban regarding the consequences of cooperating with al Qaeda. However, as the Taliban government failed to take steps against al Qaeda, the United States and its coalition partners claimed self-defense in attacking Afghanistan. The same argument—albeit problematic—has been used by U.S. decision makers to justify American attacks in Yemen and Pakistan.

MERGING LAW AND COUNTERTERRORISM

Counterterrorism conducted by civil democratic societies must necessarily be predicated on principles outlined in the Geneva Conventions. To that end, one of the most important principles established by the Geneva Conventions is the requirement to distinguish between combatants and noncombatants. The responsibility to distinguish between combatants and noncombatants is a most important principle of international law that commanders are obligated to honor; its

32 *See* Biggio, *supra*.

implementation is essential to lawful targeted killing. It is as important to targeted killing as is the principle that commanders are required to protect the innocent civilian population:

> In order to ensure respect for and protection of the civilian population and civilian objects, the Parties to the conflict shall at all times distinguish between the civilian population and combatants and between civilian objects and military objectives and accordingly shall direct their operations only against military objectives.[33]

The chart and graph below summarize principles that must be applied if the nation state is to conduct targeted killings in accordance with its international law obligations. The two, separately and collectively, emphasize the primacy of protecting innocent civilians and the obligation to limit the use of force. Re-articulated: the extraordinary military power available to the nation state must be brought to the fore in a limited, judicious manner ensuring that targets are narrowly and specifically identified and engaged. To that end, the two reinforce the commander's obligation to protect non-combatants. The importance of this responsibility cannot be sufficiently emphasized, particularly when suggestions that a flexible definition of imminence be adopted are articulated by the Obama administration. To so recommend highlights that the protection of innocent civilians is not a "given".

Targeted killing is inherently problematic; its legality and morality depend on person specific application of narrow criteria predicated on rational based decision-making. International law and the laws of war articulate a paradigm largely focused on state actors engaged in combat with other state actors. However, given the significant risks and costs associated with targeted killing principles the limits imposed on states in the traditional war paradigm must be applied to conflict between states and non- state actors. Otherwise, collateral damage will not be minimized, individuals who do not pose a viable threat will be deemed legitimate targets and principles of alternatives and proportionality will be largely ignored.

To that end, implementation of a targeted killing paradigm predicated on legality and morality is dependent on narrowly defining legitimate target and when that target is legitimate. While, admittedly, oft-repeated throughout this book that two-part analysis is at the core of a targeted killing policy conducted in accordance with principles and standards of international law and morality.

---

33 *Id.* art. 48.

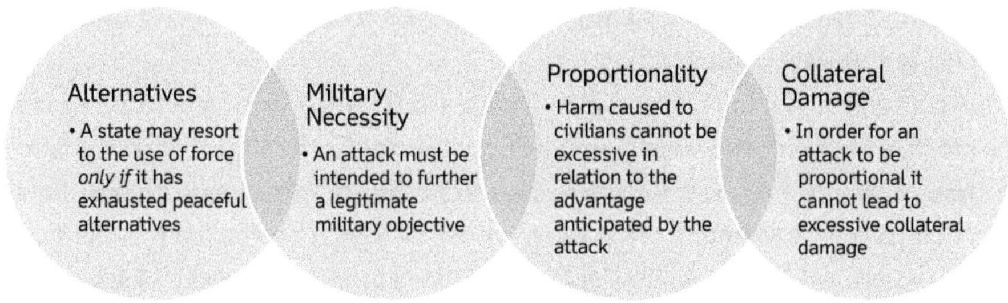

1. The civilian population shall not be the target of attacks.
2. Civilians shall enjoy protections unless they take part in attacks.
3. Indiscriminate attacks on a civilian population are prohibited.
4. Attacks shall be limited to military targets.
5. Cultural objects shall be protected.
6. Objects indispensable to a population's survival shall be protected.
7. The natural environment shall be protected. According to the 4th Hague Convention, the right to use weapons is not unlimited—weapons that cause unnecessary suffering are prohibited.

WHO POSES A THREAT?

Finally we have reached the focal point of this book: an individual can be targeted *only if*:

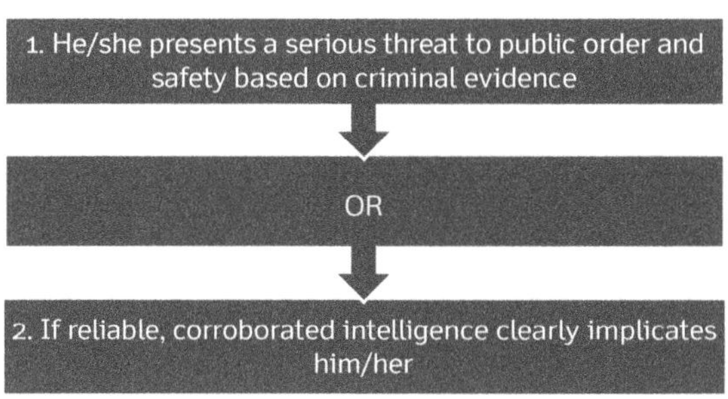

Intelligence information is corroborated when it is confirmed by at least two separate, unrelated sources. In addition, for a targeted killing to be lawful, no reasonable alternative to eliminating the threat (such as detention) is operationally viable.

According to international law, it is imperative that every effort be made to ensure that collateral damage be limited to a minimum. Therefore, when military commanders plan a targeted killing, they must do their best to avoid injury and damage to innocent civilians.[34]

Israel's targeted killing policy was articulated in its response to a petition against the practice filed with the Israel Supreme Court sitting as the High Court of Justice. In *Public Committee Against Torture v. The State of Israel*,[35] President Aharon Barak held that the targeted killing of known terrorists is legal if conducted in accordance with international law. Thus, the decision to order a terrorist's targeted killing must be rooted in the principles of proportionality, collateral damage, and alternatives.

Determining whether suicide bombers and others involved in terrorist infrastructure are legitimate targets, despite the fact that they are not soldiers in the traditional sense, is essential to analyzing whether operational counterterrorism is lawfully conducted. Presently, terrorists who take a direct role in a terrorist act are viewed as combatants (though not lawful combatants according to the laws of armed conflict) and are therefore legitimate targets. For example, this includes not just a potential suicide bomber but also anyone who plays a significant role in the suicide bomber infrastructure.

To examine targeted killing in the context of operational counterterrorism is not only to argue the law, but also to analyze the decision-making process. That process is the purpose of this book. In the following chapters, I will analyze, step by step, the process and consideration relevant to the decision to engage in a targeted killing. To do so, however, required us to travel a path that included analyzing international law, the law of war and the distinction between state actors and non- state actors.

---

[34] Otherwise they would violate the Protocol Additional to the Geneva Conventions of Aug. 12, 1949, and Relating to the Protection of Victims of International Armed Conflicts, Jun. 8, 1977.

[35] HCJ 769/02 Public Committee Against Torture v. The State of Israel [2002] (Isr.).

4

THE SOURCE, THE INTELLIGENCE COMMUNITY AND THE COMMANDER

THE LAWYER ASKS the commander a series of questions. The questions are fast, direct, and focused. Of particular interest to the lawyer is the source. After all, the conversation began when the commander said to the lawyer, "according to the source, the target poses a direct and immediate danger to national security."

Who is the source? Did you talk to the source? After all, both the commander and the lawyer know that the source—the person who provided the intelligence information—is essential to operational counterterrorism. They also know that they will never personally talk to the source, will never know his real name, and will never know his motivation for providing information to the intelligence community. That is, the decision of whether to operationally engage the identified target is triggered by an individual that only the intelligence community has interacted with. The actual contents of the conversation—whether in person or via telephone—between the source and the case officer will never be known to either the commander or the lawyer.

According to the source, who told the case officer, who told the commander (who now tells the lawyer), ***"the individual carrying the bag whose contents pose an extraordinary danger to national security is wearing blue jeans and a blue shirt . . . the individual will be at (a specific place) at (a specific time) and that will be the most opportune time to neutralize him."***

These two sentences serve as the basis for the commander's phone call to the lawyer. In other words, the information received from the source, transmitted to the commander by the case officer from the intelligence community, serves as the basis for consideration of a targeted killing. This is the essence of the discussion between the commander and the legal advisor: is the information provided by the ***source****, as analyzed by the intelligence* *community, sufficient to justify defining an otherwise innocent individual as a legitimate target?*

THE SOURCE

Communications between the commander and the case officer, and subsequently between the commander and the legal advisor, raise enormously important and significant questions that focus, necessarily and inevitably, on the source. The two most important issues are determining source reliability and information credibility, both of which are assessed exclusively by the case officer. As a member of the intelligence community, the case officer is charged with developing sources, talking with sources, and analyzing information they provide. However, the final decision whether to operationally engage lays exclusively within the domain of the commander.

In any targeted killing decision, three major questions must be answered: (1) Can the target be accurately and reliably identified? (2) Does the threat posed by the target justify an attack at that moment, or are there alternatives? (3) What is the extent of the anticipated collateral damage? Central to the first question, and thus central to all three questions, is a reliance on source-based information.

Herein lays perhaps the most complicated conundrum in operational counterterrorism: the individual who provides information to the intelligence community. Information provided by the source is essential to operational counterterrorism; that individual is, in many ways, the "eyes and ears" of the intelligence community. Timely and correct information can prevent an act of terrorism. Conversely, acting on incorrect information provided by the source can directly contribute to violating civil and political rights of an otherwise innocent individual, much less result in his death.

The intelligence community spends significant resources identifying potential sources, developing those sources, and ascertaining whether the information they provide is reliable and credible. These expenditures are justified given how much the intelligence community relies on information provided by the source. For the intelligence community, the process of identifying, recruiting, and developing sources requires intimate knowledge of the relevant targeted community's mores, norms, culture, and nuance. The opportunities to successfully recruit, much less successfully "place" a source within the relevant community, are limited. After all, terrorist organizations are well aware that such efforts by the intelligence community are essential to operational counterterrorism.

Similarly, terrorist organizations are consistently seeking to ensure their cells are not penetrated; to that end, efforts to ensure "sterility" from external penetration require vigilance, caution, and discretion. The stakes are high when the nation-state is engaged in aggressive operational counterterrorism; failure to ensure "sterility" can directly contribute to a targeted killing of a cell member. In addition to the potential loss of a cell member, targeted killings require terrorist organizations to answer two questions: who was the source that "fingered" the cell member, and how was that individual able to successfully penetrate the cell? The practical impact on a terrorist organization of a successful targeted killing is significant: it may require cancelling otherwise planned attacks; recruitment of new members when the cell is particularly vulnerable thereby heightening its vulnerability; forcing members "underground" as their identities and locations are, in all probability, exposed. Successful penetration of a terrorist cell by a source is extraordinarily disruptive; in the aftermath of a targeted killing, terrorists are inherently susceptible and deeply suspicious both of other cell members and their larger community.

A WORD OF CAUTION

The state must proceed with caution regarding information received from a source that must be held to robust and rigorous standards of examination and analysis. Because of the consequences of information received from a source, extraordinary care must be made to ensure its reliability and credibility. To that end, case officers need be sensitive to the possibility that sources will provide incorrect information, whether deliberately or not. The former occurs when the source has a "grudge-based" personal agenda regarding a particular individual; the latter occurs when communications within the cell are misinterpreted or misunderstood. Additionally, should cell members suspect someone of being a source a conscious effort will be made both to deceive the intelligence community and to "out" the suspected source by providing information best described as disinformation or misinformation.

Therefore, how intelligence agencies identify potential sources is immensely important; the risk posed by an unreliable source is immeasurable. To that end, the intelligence community must gather and analyze information received from a number of different sources. The challenge is in constructing an intelligence picture that provides decision makers with an accurate assessment both of threats posed and by whom. To that end, the burden on the intelligence community is to identify, recruit and develop multiple sources that provide information regarding general trends in a particular community and specific information with respect to a particular planned terrorist activity. To that end, information received from a source need be corroborated; additional sources of information include signal intelligence (i.e. intercepted phone conversations), visuals (i.e. satellite pictures) and other human sources.

The source is, for lack of a better term, "ratting" out someone who he knows, and is in other words a "snitch." The source is doing so for reasons of self-interest whether financial or receiving a benefit from the state. It is important to recall, when discussing targeted killing decisions, that the basis of the information comes from an individual who has a vested interest in providing information. That individual is not acting in the state's best interest; rather he is acting in his own self-interest.

This lack of objectivity, driven exclusively by presumed personal gain, must be taken into consideration when determining the reliability of the source and the information provided. Pecuniary gain or personal benefits are generally assumed to be the primary motivators in the decision to become a source.

The life of a source is extraordinarily complicated and dangerous; the risks of being "outed" are obvious, the danger consummate. As reported in the media,[1] sources—otherwise referred to as collaborators—live a life of constant risk and threat.[2] Nevertheless, the state is able to convince individuals to provide critically needed information without which operational counterterrorism, largely, cannot function. While criticism has been voiced[3] with respect to how individuals are drafted to become sources, the reality is that the relationship is mutually beneficial. One of the most important areas of inquiry is whether pressure to provide the state with information motivates sources to either provide incorrect information regarding a specific individual or to provide false information regarding an otherwise innocent individual.

Thus, skepticism must serve as a guide when assessing information provided by a source. There is, naturally, an inherent tension between the intelligence community and the "customer" or decision maker. The former has a vested interest in assuring the latter of the sources' reliability and credibility. After all, the intelligence community has drafted this individual, vetted him, and is required to "vouch" for his veracity. The decision maker has no contact with the source and

[1] http://www.guardian.co.uk/world/view-from-jerusalem-with-harriet-sherwood/2011/may/17/israel-palestinian-territories, http://www.guardian.co.uk/world/2008/jun/13/israelandthepalestinians.middleeast, http://www.nytimes.com/2012/30/world/asia/drone-war-in-pakistan-spursmilitants-to-deadlyreprisals.html?emc=eta1&_r=.

[2] While serving as a Judge in the Gaza Strip Military Court, I sat in numerous cases where defendants were accused of killing suspected Palestinian collaborators. The violence of the murders and the torture that oftentimes preceded the killing were extraordinary. In addition, the killing of suspected collaborators was occasionally committed by another Palestinian suspected of collaborating with Israel seeking to "cleanse" his name.

[3] http://www.antiwar.com/cook/?articleid=13450.

is overwhelmingly dependent on the intelligence community that, arguably, has a vested interest in assuring the "customer" regarding the source.

This raises powerful questions regarding targeted killing. When the commander (see flow chart above) relays the information provided by the case officer, his dependence on the latter is absolute. Perhaps what the commander sees in the field largely correlates to what the source (according to the case officer) has described; however there is no guarantee the individual the commander sees is the *same* person the source referenced to the case officer. While the commander is the sole decision maker the foundation on which many decisions are made—the source—is someone the commander knows nothing about.

ANALYZING INTELLIGENCE INFORMATION

One of the most challenging dilemmas in developing an operational "jigsaw puzzle" is determining whether and when the information received from a source is "actionable". Re-stated: does the information received warrant an operational response? This question is essential to the criteria-based decision-making paradigm facilitating effective operational counterterrorism whose essence is, largely, acting on the basis of imperfect information received from multiple sources. Such an approach seeks to enhance objectivity and minimize subjectivity in any decision-making process.

How does this actually work? In other words, what was the commander's basis for calling me at 3 a.m.? The "trigger" was the intelligence community's analysis that the information provided by the source was "actionable" and that the identified individual posed a sufficient threat to justify a targeted killing. Needless to say, the decision was the commander's to make. However, while the commander and the intelligence community are in distinct command structures there is clear overlap between the two functions. That said, the "division of labor" between the two results in dangerous reliance by the commander on the intelligence community. The chart below illustrates the targeted killing process; it reinforces that the source has no contact with the commander for communication is exclusively with the intelligence community. Important to recall that the source speaks in his native language; in the Israel-Palestinian model, the language of choice is Arabic. However, the language of sources language is distinct, requiring an individual trained in communicating with and delineating the substance of their message; this has been accurately depicted in TV and movies alike. That is, not only does the source speak Arabic, he is speaking "source" Arabic. The reasons for this are multifold including the great strain and pressure sources are under, the need to communicate vital information quickly, and the inherent complexity associated with providing information that endangers members of the source's own community.

The information is conveyed to the intelligence community in variety of manners including face- to -face meetings, telephone conversations or other methods of communication. Upon receipt of the information the intelligence community determines whether it is "actionable" by applying a four-part test: (1) ascertaining the source's reliability; (2) determining the viability of the information; (3) assessing the 'time relevance' of the information; (4) considering the information's credibility'. The discussion below is predicated on implementation of these criteria when a targeted killing recommendation is brought before the commander.

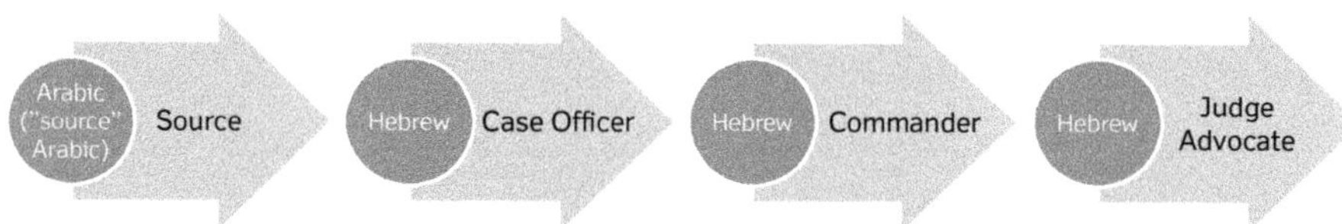

The role of the intelligence community as "linchpin" cannot be sufficiently emphasized; it recruits the source; analyzes information it receives; and then provides it to the commander; in doing so it vouches for the reliability of the source and credibility/viability of the information.

There are innumerable factors in determining whether the source has provided actionable intelligence. The question is twofold as both the source and the information must be subject to rigorous analysis. While the source might be deemed reliable and credible, the additional point of inquiry focuses on the information itself. Both questions are essential to targeted killing decisions, as the interplay between the source and the information he provides are at the heart of intelligence gathering and analysis.

In determining whether the source is reliable and credible, it is necessary to examine previous information he has provided. Doing so provides insight into past experiences but does not, obviously, guarantee that the present information is correct. In determining the reliability of the information, it is relevant to determine *how* and *when* the source received the information. The question of *how* indicates the degree to which the source has penetrated the particular terrorist organization and its hierarchy. The question of *when* suggests the time relevance of the information received.

For example, it is not enough to learn that a terrorist organization/cell is planning an attack—it is equally important to ascertain when the source learned of the plan. A targeting decision is heavily dependent on the issue of time relevance as it is directly related to the imminence of the threat posed. In order to meet tests of both legality and morality, a targeted killing decision can only be directed at an individual who poses a direct and immediate threat to national security. Otherwise the policy is predicated on retaliation and revenge, both of which violate international law and morality in armed conflict standards.

The responsibility of the intelligence community is to ensure that the source provides time-relevant information. From an operational perspective, this requires creating an infrastructure whereby the following must be institutionalized: (1) source reliability must be checked and rechecked constantly, (2) information provided by the source must be thoroughly vetted (and re-vetted), and (3) received information must be corroborated.

"Intelligence" has been defined as the collection and analysis of information relevant to development and implementation of government policy designed to enhance further national security interests by developing effective responses to threats. Critical to this definition is understanding how intelligence information is translated into operational measures. Without intelligence information, governments are unable to "connect the dots" in the best case, and in the worst case governments are unable to even identify the "dots."

Intelligence information is information that has been gathered and collected from human intelligence ("HUMINET"), from signal intelligence ("SIGINET"), or from open sources (i.e., newspapers and Internet) and subsequently analyzed. Signal intelligence is information received by a variety of strategically positioned listening devices, enabling intelligence officers to intercept conversations globally. As has been documented,[4] intercepted communications are extraordinarily important to effective operational counterterrorism. However, as the 9/11 Commission report emphasized, interception of communications is but a step in the process with respect to creating a clear—or as clear as possible—intelligence picture. After all, those listening to the intercepted conversations must be fully conversant both in the language spoken and fully familiar with the coded language of terrorists. Terrorists are fully aware that the intelligence community is engaged in a constant effort to identify them; in many ways, the terrorism-counterterrorism paradigm reflects both a race against time and a chess game.

Operational counterterrorism predicated on intelligence information based on source/sources can help justify a nation-state's engagement in aggressive, preemptive self-defense. Re-articulated, lawful self-defense against a non-state actor depends on intelligence gathering and analysis, both of which are source reliant.

[4] http://www.dailymail.co.uk/news/article-2026088/9-11-facts-Phone-terrorists-intercepted-7-weeks-attacks.html

The link between the source and preemptive self-defense in operational counter-terrorism cannot be overstated: the decision to attack a legitimate target before a planned act of terrorism occurs is largely dependent on information provided by the source.

Analyzing self-defense requires understanding the relationship between intelligence gathering and a decision to act. In seeking to objectify and legitimize self-defense, intelligence information must be evaluated according to criteria that facilitate rational based decision-making by the commander. In other words, a targeted killing recommendation must be based on made intelligence information that meets standards discussed in this chapter. Otherwise, the confluence of a flexible definition of imminence and intelligence information improperly defined as actionable will substantially increase the chances of mis-identifying an individual as a legitimate target. In addition, lowered standards will enhance the possibility of collateral damage.

The three charts below illustrate the relationship between the intelligence community and the commander; because of the commander's absolute dependence on the intelligence community the information provided must be subject to rigorous and robust standards before deemed "actionable". Adopting such a paradigm enhances operational counterterrorism predicated on the rule of law and morality in armed conflict. Failure to do so, particularly in conjunction with a flexible definition of imminence, creates a paradigm whereby direct participant and legitimate target are broadly defined. The danger in such an approach, particularly with respect to targeted killing, is significant. While the commander is the decision maker, the intelligence community's primary "customer", his decision-making is significantly influenced both by the intelligence information provided and how legitimate target is defined.

Akin to deep concerns conveyed to me by U.S. interrogators when writing "Constitutional Limits on Coercive Interrogation" the same troubling paradigm is suggested when flexible definition of imminent is offered in the context of operational counter-terrorism. For that very reason, the responsibility on the intelligence community to ensure that information provided meets the standards below is magnified. Re-articulated the cost of providing information not in accordance with the recommended criteria far outweigh the benefits regardless of arguable short-term, tactical success. That is, the long-term, strategic cost associated with intelligence information not subject to rigorous criteria prior to defined as "actionable" is significant; that cost is exacerbated when legitimate target/direct participant/imminent threat are not viewed in accordance with acceptable standards as defined by international law. The three charts below reflect the primacy of intelligence information to the commander's decision-making process and recommend structure intended to ensure its reliability, relevance and credibility.

1

- ***When*** does the actor possess information sufficient to justify taking action?

2

- ***How*** is sufficient information defined?

3

- ***What*** are the criteria for determining whether the intended victim need additional time or "another sign" prior to acting?

These three questions, in conjunction with the four- part definition and discussion below, are intended to create a structure protecting the commander from decision makers. Much in the spirit of the article Dean (then Professor) Minow and I wrote, the heavy reliance on the targeted killing paradigm—and the lack of articulated criteria regarding when its use is legitimate—demand protecting "on the ground" commanders. That protection begins with the intelligence information provided; that process begins with a burden imposed on the intelligence community regarding how information is gathered and subsequently analyzed. Otherwise, the targeted killing paradigm will quickly result in a "new Wild West".

When my phone rang at 3 a.m. a significant portion of the very short and intense conversation I had with the commander focused on the intelligence information. While the commander had spoken to the case officer, neither had met with or spoken with the source. Our dependence on the intelligence information provided and subsequently analyzed was almost absolute. The lone caveat is that the commander is the decision-maker responsible for "on the ground" assessment. Nevertheless, the importance of the intelligence information cannot be sufficiently emphasized and repeated; the need for rigorous standards in defining it "actionable" are heightened when decision-makers create a troubling paradigm reflecting flexible definitions of threats and imminence. From both an operational and legal perspective, whether at 3 a.m. or 3 p.m., the risks associated with targeted killing are too significant not to adopt the criteria below before defining intelligence information as "actionable".

Test Prong	Definition/Use
Reliable	Past experiences show the source to be a dependable provider of correct information; requires discerning whether the information is useful and accurate; demands analysis by the case officer whether the source has a personal agenda/grudge with respect to the person identified/targeted.
Viable	Is it possible that an attack could occur in accordance with the source's information?, i.e., the information provided by the source indicates a terrorist attack that could take place within the realm of the possible and feasible.
Relevant	The information has bearing on upcoming events; consider both the timeliness of the information and whether it is time sensitive, imposing the need for an immediate counterterrorism measure.
Corroborated	Another source (who meets the reliability test above) confirms the information in whole or part.

Source Criteria	
About the Source	1. What is the source's background and how does that affect the information provided? 2. Does the source have a grudge/personal "score" to settle based either on past personal or family relationship with the person the information targets or identifies?
Risks	3. What are the risks to the source if the targeted individual is targeted? • Source protection is essential to continued and effective intelligence gathering. • Protecting the source is essential both with respect to that source and additional—present or future—sources. 4. What are the risks to the source if the intelligence is made public? • Key to determining the proper forum for trying suspected terrorists.

Information from the Source	5. What information can the individual provide (premised on the operational feasibility of detention rather than authorizing a targeted killing)? 6. Does the individual possess information—to varying degrees of specificity—relevant to future acts of terrorism/individuals?
Cost-Benefit Analysis	7. What are the risks/cost-benefits if the targeted killing is delayed? • How time-relevant is the source's information? • Does it justify immediate action? • Or is the information insufficient to justify a targeted killing but significant enough to justify other measures, including detention (subject to operational considerations)?
Nature of the Activity	8. What is the nature of the suspicious activity? • Does the information suggest involvement in significant acts of terrorism justifying immediate counterterrorism measures? • Or is the information more suggestive than concrete? • In addition, if the information is indicative of minor/not harmful possible action, effective counterterrorism might suggest additional information gathering—from the same or additional source—before authorization of targeted killing.

5

THE TARGET

THE TARGET ... *what about him? Is he really a son of a bitch who deserves to have his brains blown out or he is simply in the wrong place at the wrong time? Does he even know there is a 3 a.m. phone call determining his fate? Not only does he not a have say, no one has talked to him. His thoughts—depending on who he is—range. Maybe he just wants to get home safely home to his family. Maybe he is about to hand off the explosives he has been transporting. Whoever he is, he does not want to die tonight.*

The tension in the 3 a.m. conversation is compounded by reports the commander is receiving in his earpiece regarding the target's movements. That earpiece is in his left ear. The phone receiver is in his right ear. Between his ears his brain is pounding with operational tension—do I give the "shoot to kill" order? The consequence, that someone will die, is not the core issue from his perspective. What is of the utmost importance is the safety of his troops after the mission is accomplished. He is driven by this and thus has two objectives: doing what his commanders told him to do and ensuring that his soldiers get the hell out of there safely. Every second is vital. The tone of voice in his earpiece is increasingly agitated both because the target is closer and because the more time the unit is in the field, and the closer it is to sunrise, the more dangerous it is.

The lawyer needs more information. He is sympathetic to the commander's urgings and tries to put himself in his shoes—actually his boots. The distinction between shoes and boots is critical. Real soldiers, those who shoot, bleed, sweat and spend endless nights in ambushes devoid of basic amenities (bathroom, shower, change of clothes, toilet paper if they have been away from their base for a number of days) wear boots. Shoes are anathema to them. Desk duty soldiers wear low-cut shoes. You can tell if he is a real soldier by his boots.

The lawyer needs more answers. The commander decides to press the issue ... "my friend," he tells his phone partner, "one minute to decide. Just make up your mind. One way or the other. I need to know." By now the charm school routine—which did not really exist to begin within the conversation—has been replaced by a very "now" attitude. Brusque, perhaps rude. Such is life, when someone is about to die.

The lawyer sitting in the dark of his living room understands that a decision needs to be made. He also understands that there is no one to consult with. If he says "yes," the guy (whoever he is) is dead. If he says "no," the guy lives.

OPERATIONAL COUNTERTERRORISM AND THE CRIMINAL PARADIGM

For targeted killing to meet international and constitutional law tests, and to be conducted in accordance with principles of morality in armed conflict, the decision to kill a particular individual must be predicated on criteria and process. However, to truly understand the targeted killing paradigm we must examine the individual identified a legitimate target. In analyzing the target, there are two core questions: how is a target defined as "legitimate," and when is a target defined as legitimate, indeed legitimate. The two questions must be answered from an integrated perspective, rather than as "stand-alone" silos viewed separately and distinctly.

Targeted killing is devoid of external control and review; the target is subject to extraordinary state power mitigated solely by self-imposed restraints.[1] For this very reason, every effort must be taken to ensure that the targeting decision is subject to a strict scrutiny standard within the military system.[2] The individual defined as a legitimate target, unlike a criminal suspect or defendant, is afforded neither protections nor privileges under the law. While the identified target may, indeed, pose an immediate and grave danger to state security, he is, nevertheless, devoid of any rights.

The targeted killing paradigm represents a sharp distinction between criminal law and operational counterterrorism. The criminal law regime is based on constitutionally guaranteed rights protected by law, subject to judicial review. Operational counterterrorism is best described as "in flux"; parameters, protections, and rights are largely undefined. That same distinction applies when comparing the law of war[3] and operational counterterrorism; the limits of operational

---

[1] This is an issue I have addressed elsewhere; *See, e.g.*, Amos N. Guiora, *Determining a Legitimate Target: The Dilemma of the Decision Maker*, 47 TEXAS INT'L L.J. (forthcoming 2012), *available at* http://ssrn.com/abstract=1905130. In addition, see www.thedailybeast.com—interview-with-harold-koh-obama-s-defender-of-drone-strikes.html, for Legal Advisor to the Department of State Harold Koh's opinion on the need for criteria and process in targeted killing.

[2] *See* Gregory S. McNeal, *The U.S. Practice of Collateral Damage Estimation and Mitigation*, November 9, 2011, *available at* http://papers.ssrn.com/sol3/papers.cfm?abstract_id=1819583. (McNeal's article provides an excellent and thorough analysis of U.S. military considerations in air-to-surface operations.)

[3] Please see earlier discussion regarding the Geneva Conventions, the Hague Convention and the U.N. Charter

counterterrorism are largely subject to the nation-state's self-imposed restraints.[4] The distinction between these paradigms is particularly relevant when discussing the target. For example, under the traditional laws of war, a soldier is accorded status and protection. That is in contrast to the amorphousness that characterizes status and protections in operational counterterrorism. This murkiness is particularly acute when determining whether a particular individual is, indeed, a legitimate target and can be the lawful target of a targeted killing. Unlike the traditional criminal law paradigm where the rights of the individual transitioning from suspect to defendant are fully guaranteed, the operational counterterrorism paradigm affords no such protections.

For example, in the criminal system, an individual arrested on suspicion of involvement in criminal activity is guaranteed rights ranging from Miranda warnings, to the right to counsel at trial, to the right to appeal his conviction; in addition, prosecutorial decisions regarding the individual are subject to judicial review that may result in judicial intervention. Furthermore, unless superseding national security or sensitive privacy concerns prevail, criminal trials are open to the public and therefore subject to media and public scrutiny alike. That transparency, so vital to protecting individual rights, represents a clear demarcation line between operational counterterrorism and the criminal law paradigm. After all, operational counterterrorism can be described as conducted in the "back alleys with dark shadows" whereas the criminal law is largely subject to the glare of the hot lights of the media.

As depicted in television shows[5] and movies,[6] individual rights are the essence of the criminal law process. Similarly, individual rights similarly apply to soldiers captured in the traditional war paradigm. After all, a captured soldier—fighting on behalf of a nation-state while carrying his weapon openly with visible insignia and subject to a recognized chain of command—may not be questioned by his captors and must only state his name, rank, and serial number. Furthermore, his captors may not prosecute a captured soldier unless he has committed either a war crime or a crime while in captivity.

Both the criminal law and the laws of war are predicated on a complex balancing paradigm guaranteeing the nation-state the right to protect itself while imposing an obligation to protect the individual who, until arrest or capture, endangered the state. In other words, criminal law and laws of war are predicated on the right to self-defense tempered by the requirement to protect the individual once he no

---

[4] See Aharon Barak, President (retired), Supreme Court of Israel, address at the Fulbright Convention, *Comparative Law, Originalism, and the Role of the Judge in a Democracy: A Reply to Justice Scalia* (January 29, 2006).

[5] See, *Law and Order* series and *CSI* as prominent examples.

[6] See, *To Kill a Mockingbird*, *12 Angry Men*, *Presumed Innocent*, and *My Cousin Vinny* as prominent examples.

longer poses a threat. This clarity, based on laws and conventions, is largely missing in operational counterterrorism, particularly regarding the legal limits of state power. While the nation-state has literally an unlimited arsenal at its availability, the operative inquiry is whether, and how, person-specific operational counterterrorism is articulated and implemented.

In the criminal law paradigm, law enforcement often spontaneously respond to a crime that is occurring or is about to occur; conversely, a targeted killing reflects a planned military operation representing the confluence of intelligence gathering, analysis, and operational decision making. In the criminal law paradigm, the target is the perpetrator to whom law enforcement is responding, whereas the target in a targeted killing is an individual who the intelligence community has been tracking over the course of time and has determined that, in order to prevent a particular act of terrorism, the individual must be killed. The distinction between the two paradigms is enormous: in the criminal law model, the decision to engage is made "on the spot" by a law enforcement officer. In the terrorism paradigm, the target has been defined as posing a threat based on intelligence gathering and analysis *prior* to the decision to operationally engage the individual.

Once the intelligence community recommends that the individual be killed—predicated on gathered intelligence information that has been analyzed—the decision is in the commander's hands. However, unlike the criminal law paradigm the commander in the targeted killing paradigm does not act independent of the intelligence community and does not necessarily see the individual committing the act at the basis of the decision to engage.

To summarize, in the criminal law paradigm the perpetrator is observed by the law enforcement agent committing a crime, whereas in the targeted killing paradigm the target is not necessarily observed committing an act of terrorism, for the model is predicated on preventive action based on intelligence information and analysis.

THE RULE OF LAW

A targeted killing paradigm conducted in accordance with the rule of law imposes in the nation-state the obligation to respect the four principles below:

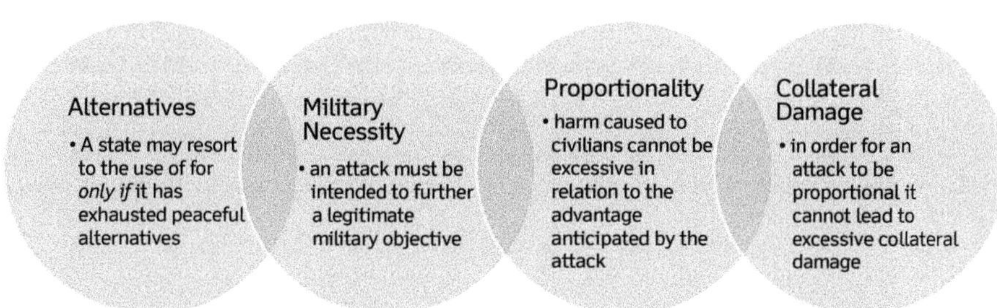

These concepts become stark reality in the targeting discussion; it is where the application of international law and morality[7] to operational decision making meet. Unlike the criminal law and law of war paradigms, the operational counterterrorism paradigm pits the nation-state, with panoply of power, against an individual. While the individual may belong to an organization, a "lone wolf" similarly may pose a clear and specific threat to national security. That is, the individual defined as a legitimate target may be just that: a single person unaffiliated with any organization. Subject to circumstances and conditions, both the lone wolf and those belonging to groups may be defined as legitimate targets.

The over-arching question is what degree of threat does the individual pose and how best to minimize the threat or neutralize the individual. Answering that question requires understanding *who* the target is and *why* they are a target. However, before doing so, it is important to emphasize the extraordinary importance of the four international law principles above. A lawful targeting decision requires strict application of all four principles; international law cannot tolerate an "and/or" implementation model. While this requirement undoubtedly burdens nation-state decision-making, application of an alternative model would result in violations of the rule of law. By graphic analogy, it is the difference between commanders teaching their soldiers how to kill as compared to being killers; the former is the essence of war, the latter is a clear violation of laws of war and international law.

Application of international law standards to operational counterterrorism protects the potential target. Without self-imposed restraint, the definition of legitimate target would be extraordinarily broad, subject neither to limits nor careful decision- making. Undoubtedly, a valid argument can be made that this requirement imposes an undue burden on the nation-state providing an undesirable benefit to the potential target. Those who argue international law imposes a unilateral limit on how the nation-state conducts operational counterterrorism have suggested this argument.[8]

According to this theory, in a zero-sum analysis, the potential target is actually handed an undue advantage given the limits the nation-state self-imposes in accordance with external standards and criteria. There is, without doubt, credibility to this argument: targeting decisions that reflect respect for standards and criteria are, *indeed,* intended to protect the potential target from an undue exercise of state power. In that context, the decision by the nation-state to respect

---

[7] *See, e.g.*, BRIAN OREND, THE MORALITY OF WAR (Broadview Press 2006). I also recommend reading Megan M. Thompson, *Moral and ethical dilemmas in Canadian Forces military operations: Qualitative and descriptive analyses of commanders' operational experiences*, Defense R&D Canada, Toronto (October 2008).

[8] *See, e.g.*, Ted Lapkin, *Does Human Rights Law Apply to Terrorists?* MIDDLE EAST QUARTERLY 3 (Fall 2004).

international law is to the target's advantage. Conversely, an individual identified as a legitimate target by a nation-state that does not respect international law and/or self-imposed restraint is at an extraordinary disadvantage.

Adoption of criteria-based targeting decisions directly contributes to more effective operational counterterrorism, but does not guarantee mistakes will not be made and innocent people not killed. Targeting decisions predicated on a broad, sometimes extraordinarily broad, definition of legitimate target results both in significant collateral damage and "blowback" enhancing recruitment to terrorist organizations. In addition to international law considerations there are, then, practical considerations for the nation-state to create and apply criteria-based process.

To that extent, the Obama administration's stated policy[9] that an individual in the immediate vicinity of a suspected terrorist is likely to belong to a terrorist organization and is, therefore, a legitimate target is most disturbing. That policy enables the CIA to claim[10] that U.S. drone policy under the Obama administration has not resulted in collateral damage. Such a claim suggests individuals killed by the United States in Pakistan, Afghanistan, Somalia, Yemen, and other countries where the drone policy is implemented are legitimate targets, regardless of their involvement in terrorism. That is an extraordinarily broad, and frankly, dangerous definition of legitimate target akin to "guilt by association."

Application of "guilt by association" or "round up the usual suspects" in the targeting paradigm is profoundly different than in the criminal law paradigm: while "round up the usual suspects" results in widespread and unjustified arrests, "guilt by association" in the targeted killing paradigm results in the deaths of individuals whose involvement in terrorism has not been carefully assessed nor ascertained. That is the significance of the Obama administration's policy; it is the antithesis of lawful, aggressive self-defense that must be at the core of a targeted killing/drone policy.

TARGET DETERMINATION

With that, we turn our attention to the target. Who is he? How did he become a target? What is the significance of becoming a target? What actions can an individual take to convince the nation-state that he is not involved in terrorism and,

---

9 John O. Brennan, Assistant to the President for Homeland Security and Counterterrorism, Strengthening our Security by Adhering to our Values and Laws, Address at Harvard Law School (Sept. 16, 2011) (transcript available at http://www.whitehouse.gov/the-press-office/2011/09/16/remarks-john-o-brennan-strengthening-our-security-adhering-our-values-an).

10 *See* Scott Shane, *C.I.A. is Disputed on Civilian Toll in Drone Strikes*, NEW YORK TIMES (Aug. 11, 2011), *available at* http://www.nytimes.com/2011/08/12/world/asia/12drones.html?_r=1&hp.

therefore, not a legitimate target? When do the actions of the target justify killing him? Important to recall the mere fact an individual has been defined as a legitimate target does not automatically mean he must be killed. That said, the reality of operational counterterrorism is that once an individual as a legitimate target, he "enters" a category whereby chances of a targeted killing are significant.

It is precisely because of the extraordinary ramifications of the "target" designation must be based on his actions alone. That is why the Obama administration's policy is so deeply troubling. Given the obvious impact of a targeted killing decision, implementation must be dependent on an extraordinarily robust examination of all information regarding that individual. Otherwise, targeting decisions are standard-less, bordering on group affiliation, rather than individual actions. The intelligence community and operational decision makers must focus their individual and combined efforts on determining whether the individual defined as a legitimate target is, indeed, a legitimate target. Focusing on the individual is the most effective rebuttal to deep and justified concerns that have been raised regarding targeted killing.[11]

Critics have focused on different aspects of targeted killing, ranging from the philosophical[12] to the legal[13] to the practical;[14] their concern is both legitimate and understandable. That criticism must be divided into two distinct categories: those who argue the state has a limited right to engage in self-defense but believe that targeted killing is inherently illegal, and those who believe that targeted killing can be legal but disagree with how the policy is implemented. With respect to the first category, discussion addressing the target will, in all probability, not convince them of the policy's legality. However, highlighting the state's obligation to narrowly define legitimate target will allay concerns relevant to the second category provided the state establishes a targeted killing paradigm predicated on a criteria-based analysis regarding the threat posed by the target. Failure to do so will all but inevitably drive the second category of skeptics—if not critics—into the first category.

Re-articulated: those opposed to aggressive, proactive self-defense will, in all likelihood, remain opposed to targeted killing; deep concerns articulated by others may be mitigated if convinced that targeting individuals is, indeed, individual

[11] see chapter 2

[12] *See* Mary Ellen O'Connell, *Unlawful Killing with Combat Drones: A Case Study of Pakistan, 2004–2009* (Notre Dame Legal Studies Paper No. 09-43, 2010), *available at* http://papers.ssrn.com/sol3/papers.cfm?abstract_id=1501144.

[13] *See id. See also* American Civil Liberties Union, *Targeted Killings* (Apr. 28, 2010) http://www.aclu.org/human-rights-national-security/targeted-killings.

[14] *See* Adam Entous et al., *U.S. Tightens Drone Rules*, WALL STREET JOURNAL (Nov. 4, 2011) http://online.wsj.com/article/SB10001424052970204621904577013982672973836.html?mod=wsj_share_tweet.

based. To meet standards of morality and legality the targeting decision must be based on rigorous standards. This requires the intelligence community[15] gather, analyze, and provide information conclusively indicating a specific individual poses significant threat to national security. To that extent, there must be a "match" between the individual target and threat to national security based on rigorous assessment of *that* individual's actions.

When the commander called me, the individual identified by the intelligence community as the legitimate target was walking and carrying a bag; the relevant question was whether the contents in the bag matched the description provided by the source. Given the nature of the alleged material in the bag, the commander determined approaching the individual was operationally unfeasible and presented a risk he was unwilling to impose on his unit, a decision I fully concurred with. Therefore, the decision whether to engage would, ultimately, be based on a variety of factors based on information provided by the source, analysis by the intelligence community, and assessment by the commander. The decision to engage does not include actual physical contact with the individual identified as the target. It is that "distance" between the decision maker and the target that is particularly problematic because the impetus for operational engagement does not come from the commander but from the intelligence community.

Though law enforcement is subject to public criticism, particularly regarding excessive use of force,[16] the public has a clearer understanding of the decision-making process.[17] That certainty does not apply to targeted killing, partly because of a lack of government transparency regarding how and when an individual is defined as a legitimate target.[18]

When confronted with targeting dilemmas, my focus was to understand the threat posed by the targeted individual as articulated by the intelligence community. However, as previously discussed, I did not have direct communication with the intelligence community and was dependent on the commander's interpretation of his conversation with the intelligence community. Our conversation was exclusively predicated on information he directly received from the intelligence community focusing on whether the individual defined as a legitimate target was

---

15 see chapter 4

16 For a recent example, *see* Matt Taibbi, *UC Davis Pepper-Spray Incident Reveals Weakness Up Top*, TAIBBLOG (Nov. 22, 2011), *available at* http://www.rollingstone.com/politics/blogs/taibblog/uc-davis-pepper-spray-incident-reveals-weakness-up-top-20111122.

17 *See* Connie L. McNeely, *Perceptions of the Criminal Justice System: Television Imagery and Public Knowledge in the United States*, 3 JOURNAL OF CRIMINAL JUSTICE AND POPULAR CULTURE (1995), *available at* http://www.albany.edu/scj/jcjpc/vol3is1/perceptions.html.

18 *See* A.C.L.U. *Targeted Killings*, supra.

the right individual. Simply put, we asked ourselves whether the individual in the commander's scope was the person identified by the intelligence community.

What had that individual done in order to be categorized as such? Needless to say, over the years I have replayed this conversation countless times in an effort to better understand the extraordinarily broad range of factors involved in the targeted killing decision. Of particular interest is what led the intelligence community to conclude that the person presented to me as a legitimate target was indeed a legitimate target. According to information available to the intelligence community—whether from single or multiple sources—the individual was carrying a bag, the contents of which presented an immediate and grave danger to national security. On the face of it, that information justified defining the individual as a legitimate target; after all, the basis of the policy is to engage in aggressive self-defense intended to protect the nation-state.

The question was whether the individual's actions justified, in addition to the available intelligence information, defining him as a legitimate target. To properly answer that question we needed to carefully break down, step by step, the information presented to the commander, match that against the policy's stated goals, and then subject that two-part analysis to a rigorous examination of international law and morality in armed conflict. It is important to recall that for a threat to be considered sufficiently viable in the context of targeted killing, it must be deemed imminent *narrowly defined;* otherwise, a targeted killing decision is truly criteria-less, devoid of restraint and standards.

To reiterate: the commander and I knew, according to the source(s),[19] that the individual, identified as the target, carried a bag with material that potentially endangered national security. It was not made clear to me whether the individual knew what was in the bag; in other words, could he have been a courier used by a terrorist organization for the purpose of transporting material without knowing its contents? The answer is yes, though the obvious follow-up question is how an individual becomes a courier for a terrorist organization: is it by chance that the individual is requested to transport material? Or is he a valued and trusted member of that organization? Resolving those questions is essential in determining whether an individual is a legitimate target. The dilemma deepens then, requiring resolution of whether an individual can be defined as legitimate predicated on actions alone, regardless of intent and knowledge.

To answer requires determining under what conditions the targeted killing policy may be implemented: what act—or potential act—constitutes a legitimate

[19] Important to recall that the commander referred to *a* source. Israeli intelligence officials have repeatedly stressed, in private conversations, that targeted killing recommendations are based on multiple sources rather than a single source.

justification for the nation-state to kill an individual? To highlight the issue, the "standard" (the quotation is deliberate as I am skeptical that a standard exists) established by the Obama administration justifies killing an individual based on merely being in the presence of a suspected terrorist, devoid of an intent requirement regarding future terrorist activity. This "standard" suggests that the definition applied in the United States regarding a legitimate target is significantly broader than that tolerated by international law. It is, frankly, significantly broader than what I applied when the commander requested my operational legal advice.

To circle back, my phone conversation with the commander focused on the target; however, we also discussed the source, the competence and training of the commander's unit, and the commander's assessment of relevant field conditions including operational alternatives and possible collateral damage. Focusing on the target during our conversation[20] required I receive the commander's insight into the target's movements, actions, and conduct. While the intelligence community's recommendation served as the impetus for the conversation, the commander's assessment was of extraordinary importance in my decision-making process.

The intelligence community's request to conduct the targeted killing was predicated on their assessment of the source's reliability and credibility. That, however, did not guarantee—under any condition—that that the individual observed by the commander in real time was the target. The mere fact that the intelligence community believed a "match" existed was not sufficient for the commander to operationally engage the individual or for me to respond affirmatively to the question the commander posed. The requirement to articulate and implement a strict scrutiny paradigm demands the intelligence community's recommendation be subject to rigorous analysis by "boots on the ground."

The commander had the advantage of seeing and watching the individual and that insight, based on years of experience and training in operational counterterrorism, was of extraordinary importance. Unlike the intelligence community, whose recommendation was based on conversations with a source and subsequent analysis of information, the commander, in the field, and could provide an unblemished account of the targeted individual's conduct. The efforts were intended to ascertain whether the individual's actions were in accordance with information provided by the intelligence community. Clearly, this is an imperfect assessment model because the commander was not provided information regarding distinguishable characteristics or traits suggesting suspicious behavior. The information identifying the target did not dramatically distinguish him from countless

[20] The reader will note that my use of the word "conversation" refers to a terse, highly focused, professional exchange between two senior military officers determining whether to authorize the killing of another human being.

others who carry bags, wear blue jeans and blue shirts. However, the question was whether those facts, in conjunction with the target's location, sufficiently identified the individual as a legitimate target.

SUMMARY OF TARGET DETERMINATION

While other factors were relevant to the decision-making process, our primary effort was seeking to ascertain whether the identified individual was, indeed, the target. Or, was this simply a "wrong place, wrong time" scenario? Particularly vexing was how limited the information was; deeply troubling was the potential threat the individual posed. That dilemma, or perhaps dichotomy, is at the heart of targeted killing. The chart highlights questions relevant to determining whether and when the target is, in fact, legitimate:

Target Determination

1. Who is the "target" of the source's information?
   - What is the person's role in the terrorist organization?
   - How will detention affect that organization, short term and long term alike?
   - What insight can the source provide regarding "impact"?·
2. What are the risks/cost-benefits if the targeted killing is delayed?
   - How time relevant is the source's information?
   - Does it justify immediate action?
   - Or is the information insufficient to justify a targeted killing but significant enough to justify other measures, including detention (subject to operational considerations)?
3. What is the nature of the suspicious activity?
   - Does the information suggest involvement in significant acts of terrorism justifying immediate counterterrorism measures?
   - Or is the information more suggestive than concrete?
   - In addition, if the information is indicative of minor/not harmful possible action, effective counterterrorism might suggest additional information gathering—from the same or additional source—before authorization of targeted killing.
4. What information can the individual provide (premised on the operational feasibility of detention rather than authorizing a targeted killing)?
5. Does the individual possess information—to varying degrees of specificity—relevant to future acts of terrorism/individuals?

Implementation of a person-specific process is essential to lawful operational counterterrorism paradigm. Identifying the "who" (the legitimate target) is but half of the analysis. Determining "when" is of no less importance and significance. The burden on the nation-state is to ensure that the "banality of evil", as brilliantly described by Hannah Arendt[21], does not enter soldiers' lexicon—philosophically or practically—in the field of battle. Therefore, the proposal in this book is that every targeted killing decision be subject to strict scrutiny and criteria.

Needless to say, this requirement imposes significant burden on the nation-state; that is, however, the essence of lawful and moral operational counterterrorism. The challenge, as discussed below, is determining how broadly the "target" is to be defined; with that, we turn our attention to Operation Cast Lead.

OPERATION CAST LEAD

By way of quick review: as a result of the 1967 Six Day War, Israel occupied the West Bank, Gaza Strip, Golan Heights, Sinai Peninsula, and East Jerusalem: a military government was established in both the Gaza Strip and the West Bank. The 1993 Oslo Peace Process was intended to establish a Palestinian State (West Bank and Gaza Strip); in accordance with the Oslo Agreement, the Palestinian Authority (PA) was created (stepping into the shoes of the Palestine Liberation Organization), and the Israel Defense Forces (IDF) significantly re-deployed in the Gaza Strip and in a limited manner in the West Bank. In August 2005, then-Prime Minister Sharon decided Israel would unilaterally withdraw from the Gaza Strip. In 2006, Hamas defeated the PA in open and free elections in the Gaza Strip; shortly thereafter, Hamas began to regularly fire Qassam (crude, short-range artillery) and Garde missiles into southern Israel. Given the 40-kilometer radius of the missiles, 700,000 Israelis were under daily threat of attack. In December 2008, the government of then-Prime Minister Olmert initiated Operation Cast Lead. The stated purpose of the military operation was to "restore the principle of deterrence in Southern Israel."[22]

On Saturday, December 27, 2008, Israeli military aircraft attacked a Palestinian police graduation ceremony. For the next 22 days, the IDF conducted an aggressive military campaign largely based on aerial attacks with infantry and armored corps involvement.[23] International public opinion largely condemned the Israel

[21] Hannah Arendt, Eichmann in Jerusalem: A Report on the Banality of Evil (Penguin Books 1994) (1963).

[22] Paul Wood, *Analysis: Operation Miscast Lead?* BBC News (Mar. 13, 2009), http://news.bbc.co.uk/2/hi/7940624.stm.

[23] *Operation Cast Lead,* GlobalSecurity.org, http://www.globalsecurity.org/military/world/war/operation-cast-lead.htm (last visited Dec. 1, 2011).

operation.[24] The Goldstone Report, mandated by the United Nations, heavily criticized Israel;[25] in particular, Israel was criticized for violating the international law principle of proportionality. Opponents of Israel's actions highlighted sharp differences between the number of Israelis killed by missiles before the Operation began and the number of Gazans killed during the Operation,[26] and the significant property damage caused by IDF attacks in Gaza viewed as disproportionate to property damage suffered by Israelis.[27]

Regarding legitimate target, Israel unilaterally re-articulated the definition. Rather than applying the traditional person-specific paradigm, Operation Case Lead reflected a significant broadening of the term. The shift was premised on conviction that firing thousands missiles into Israel over the course of two years[28] required an infrastructure whereby *all* involved posed a significant threat to national security. Re-articulated: to effectively prevent the firing of Qassam and Garde missiles, aggressive self-defense justified broadening the definition of legitimate target to more effectively protect the civilian population.

Below are the four categories defined as legitimate targets in Operation Cast Lead:

1) Individuals involved in making missiles (in factories located in the Gaza Strip);
2) Individuals involved in smuggling missiles from Egypt through tunnels leading into the Gaza Strip;
3) Individuals involved in firing missiles into Israel;[29]
4) Individuals providing support to Hamas, including the willing use of their land for purposes of missile firing.

This change, needless to say, was significant and controversial largely because support for Hamas was now categorized as a legitimate target category equivalent with active involvement in terrorism. For this model to be applied in accordance with international law principles previously discussed implies redefinition of proportionality. To wit: the power and force of the nation-state is inherently

[24] *See* Nahum Barnea, Op-Ed, *Goldstone Aftershocks*, NEW YORK TIMES (Apr. 10, 2011), *available at* http://www.nytimes.com/2011/04/11/opinion/11iht-edbarnea11.html. *See also* Stephen R. Shalom, *Unjust and Illegal: The Israel Attack on Gaza*, 8 LOGOS: A JOURNAL OF MODERN SOCIETY AND CULTURE (2009).

[25] Goldstone subsequently sought to retract the Report (Richard Goldstone, *Reconsidering the Goldstone Report on Israel and war crimes*, Op-Ed, WASHINGTON POST (Apr. 1, 2011), *available at* http://www.washingtonpost.com/opinions/reconsidering-the-goldstone-report-on-israel-and-war-crimes/2011/04/01/AFg111JC_story.html); his clumsy and largely unexplained efforts backtracking from the Report were rejected by members of the Committee and dismissed by the broader international human rights community.

[26] http://www.btselem.org/download/20090909_cast_lead_fatalities_eng.pdf; http://www.jewishvirtuallibrary.org/jsource/Terrorism/IDFvictimsOCL.html.

[27] http://www.ict.org.il/Portals/0/Articles/ICT-Hamas_Casualties_Operation_Cast_Lead.pdf.

[28] For information on the number of rockets fired into Israel, *see FACTBOX—Hamas's Arsenal of Rockets*, REUTERS (Jan. 6, 2009), http://www.reuters.com/article/2009/01/06/idUSL6529388.

[29] The missiles are fired by either by handheld rocket launchers or easily transportable rocket launchers; in both cases the firing process (set-up to firing) is extremely brief suggesting significant tactical advantage to those firing

disproportionate to that of the non-state actor. The former has an extraordinary arsenal, far superior in quantity and quality, to that of the latter. To that end, the more correct question is *how* the nation-state uses the weapons it possesses, with the understanding that proportionality is, largely, a misnomer in the context of operational counterterrorism.

The more appropriate question is whether force used is proportionate to the threat posed with recognition that force available to the nation-state is *inherently* disproportionate to that available to the non-state actor. With respect to the firing of 10,000 missiles two important decisions were made: the act threatened national security, and all involved in the missile infrastructure were legitimate targets. Unlike the Obama administration's "likely" standard, the Israeli model required *actual* involvement, expanded to include passive support. In other words, a legitimate target need not be the individual firing the missile or planning a suicide bombing; a legitimate target, in accordance with Operation Cast Lead, could be the individual facilitating and providing passive support for terrorism.[30]

FINAL WORD

According to the source in my scenario, the "target" would be carrying the bag; there was no indication—at least none articulated to me—that he would be using the material in the bag. Does that define him as a "courier" and, therefore, not a legitimate target? An analogy to the missile-firing infrastructure suggests actions comparable to the individual smuggling missiles from Egypt who as Operation Cast Lead made clear is a legitimate target. A courier, in a broader sense, is comparable to a conduit nation. For example: the 2006 conflict between Hezbollah and Israel was significantly facilitated by Syria; [31] missiles fired by Hezbollah into Israel were supplied by Iran and transported *through* Syria.[32] Whether Syria's actions were akin to an act of war is a legitimate question; without their critical role, Iran would have had to develop a significantly more circuitous, complicated, and perhaps operationally unfeasible infrastructure for supplying Hezbollah.

The decision, regarding the target, required us to not only ascertain the validity and reliability of the intelligence information (without talking or meeting with the source), but also to determine whether a courier was a legitimate target. The analysis demanded determining not only whether the information provided was sufficient but also to resolve whether the presumed, as reported by the source, actions of the alleged target met a broad standard of self-defense. Important to recall

---

30 For further reading on this issue, *see* Amos N. Guiora & David J. Luban, *Was the Gaza Campaign Legal?*, 31 ABA NATIONAL SECURITY LAW REPORT 1 (2009).

31 *See* Mitchell Bard, *Potential Threats to Israel: Syria*, JEWISH VIRTUAL LIBRARY (Nov. 3, 2011).

32 *Id.*

targeted killing reflects aggressive, proactive self-defense; the question, therefore, was whether the alleged degree of involvement by the target justified killing him.

The dilemma was not simple. My assertion that person-specific, criteria-driven targeted killing is legal, moral, and effective is but "half the battle"; the question is in the policy's application. While the commander and I were weighing our options, he was very focused on the actions and movements of the target, essential to our decision-making process. The target did not conduct himself in a manner suggesting he was suspicious the IDF was observing him, unlike others whose conduct in the criminal law paradigm suggested culpability, therefore "tipping off" law enforcement. The target in question was seemingly oblivious that he was possibly seconds from his death. While that was not the key factor in our decision-making process, it was a fact taken into consideration. As has been documented elsewhere,[33] individuals involved in terrorism oftentimes assume the nation-state is aware of their activities, tracking their movements; to that end, someone aware his movements are monitored conducts himself accordingly whether that involves changing addresses frequently or moving furtively. That was not the case before us, as the target's actions did not, independent of the information provided by the source, raise the commander's suspicion. However, that does not inherently mean the target was not a legitimate target, but it was a relevant consideration.

Complicating our dilemma—with respect to the specific target—was our absolute dependence on the intelligence community. The intelligence information indicated a significant threat to national security; while some of what the commander saw confirmed the report received, there were sufficient "holes" to raise doubts in our minds. While operational counterterrorism implies killing individuals who pose a direct threat to national security, strict standards of legality and morality require the analysis carefully consider "in the field" circumstances and conditions. The commander must assess the target's actions, and conduct; otherwise, targeted killing will result in operational counterterrorism that violates international law.

At 3 a.m., neither the commander nor I were convinced the individual was actually the target. In addition, it is an open question whether a courier is a legitimate target. That is not to say that under certain circumstances, perhaps reflecting greater certainty than we were confronted with, a courier is legitimate. In the dilemma at the heart of this book, the circumstances did not meet what can best be described as a strict scrutiny test that, the commander and I implemented.

---

[33] *See* MALCOLM W. NANCE, TERRORIST RECOGNITION HANDBOOK: A PRACTITIONER'S MANUAL FOR PREDICTING AND IDENTIFYING TERRORIST ACTIVITIES (CRC Press 2008).

6

THE PRACTICALITIES OF TARGETED KILLING

THE WORD "PRACTICALITY" is, perhaps, off-putting when analyzing whether or not when discussing the killing of another human being. The word was deliberately chosen, after much thought, because it accurately describes an essential component of the decision-making process. It is insufficient to determine that the target is a "legitimate" target; while required by international law, domestic law, and ethical considerations, the decision must reflect *additional* analysis going beyond the legal and moral. Specifically, practical considerations are necessary in order to ensure that the decision is in accordance with national interests, however defined.

The decision-making regarding a particular individual must be viewed through a multiple-lens approach extending beyond that person. By analogy: in teaching criminal procedure, I recommend that students examine criminal acts through a "multiple audience theory." Rather than examining the crime through the lenses of actor and victim exclusively, I suggest their actions be examined in addition to law enforcement, the judiciary, the prosecutor, the victim's family, the larger public, and the defense bar. This approach—a broad examination of the impact of a specific targeted killing—is the essence of this chapter.

A targeted killing has a dramatic effect beyond the specific, targeted individual; decision-making must reflect sensitivity to local, regional, national and international reactions and criticism. In using the word "practicality," my reference is to a 10-point checklist that analyzes effectiveness, cost-benefit considerations, geopolitics, and domestic politics. The decision-making tree, essential to operational counterterrorism, must reflect strategic assessment no less than tactical assessment. The saying that a tree falling in the forest is not heard beyond the forest is, in many cases, the exact opposite of the impact of a specific targeted killing. Quite often, the noise emanating from a particular "hit" is so loud that it is as if the entire forest has been felled. The questions that decision makers face in the aftermath of a particular hit—regardless of its noise—requires careful analysis before the attack in order to ensure the ripples emanating from a targeted killing do not turn into a tsunami.

Articulating and implementing policy is essential to operational counterterrorism; however, policy alone will not guarantee success or effectiveness, either in the short or long term. However, the failure to create and articulate a policy guarantees that operational counterterrorism will not be effective, moral, or legal. Development of a coherent and cohesive "mission statement" when undertaking a particular operation is essential; however, a particular mission must reflect adherence to a larger policy rather than a "lurching" from event to event without significant forethought and foresight. Because of the impact of targeted killing—beyond that of the individual and his immediate family—the decision-making tree *must* reflect emphasis on significant, additional factors. There must be recognition that additional factors require the input of decision makers extending beyond the "on the ground" commander. That is, given the significance of targeted killing, both the policy and its specific implementation require careful analysis of the decisions' impact by a wide range of individuals. Otherwise, the fallout may well be enormous, if not irreversible. *That* is the essence of practicality.

In previous chapters, targeted killing was examined from the perspective of the source, the commander, and the target. In this chapter, targeted killing is examined from additional, more strategic perspectives. Doing so requires extending the circle of decision makers beyond "on the ground" commanders and their advisors; the rationale for this requirement is the significance of a specific targeted killing decision. Operational counterterrorism in general and targeted killing in particular reflect a meeting of law, policy, effectiveness, and morality at a complicated four-way intersection. These four invite tension and discord, practically and intellectually, because distinct decision-making groups are involved in the process.

The criteria-based approach to targeted killing is significantly enhanced if national decision makers subject operational counterterrorism to a checklist approach akin to what on-the-ground commanders use. Given the dramatic fallout from operational counterterrorism operations gone awry, the positives of a criteria-based checklist significantly outweigh perceived negatives. To that end, the checklist (below) is intended for national decision makers. Needless to say, the issues are significantly different than the checklist proposed for "on-the-ground" commanders. The checklist reflects the geopolitical realities of targeted killing (as distinct from the operational considerations), from the perspective of domestic

Ten-Point Criteria Based Checklist	
"Past" Questions	1) What have been the local community reactions to previous targeted killings?
	2) What has been the international community's reactions to previous targeted killings?
	3) Does recent terrorist activity/lack of terrorist activity justify implementing the policy?
Predictive Questions	4) Are there current political circumstances that preclude conducting a targeted killing?
	5) What are the predicted/expected reactions to a proposed targeted killing?
	6) What are the predicted/expected consequences if an otherwise legitimate targeted killing is not conducted?
	7) What are the expected/predicted geo-political ramifications of a particular killing?
Legal Questions	8) Do recent legislative or judicial decisions impact executive branch decision-making with respect to the targeted killing policy?
	9) What weight is ascribed to sovereignty considerations?
Other	10) Is domestic public pressure a consideration [particularly in the aftermath of a terrorist attack)?

and international considerations alike. While different nations have distinct political, social, cultural, legal, and judicial realities, the checklist is sufficiently broad to reflect those inherent differences.

One word of disclaimer: the checklist is predicated on decision makers having determined that targeted killing as a policy is legal, moral, and effective and that specific categories of legitimate target have been defined.

Later in this chapter I will revisit this 10-point checklist and further discuss why each point is critical in defining a legitimate target. Before doing so, however, six specific targeted killing decisions will be examined with the intent to put "meat on the bones". These examples are illustrative of the tension between strategic and tactical decision-making regarding particular individuals and are instructive with respect to application of "self-defense."

Example #1:
It is widely rumored that during the course of the 1982 Israel-Lebanon War, Yasser Arafat, the then-Chairman of the Palestine Liberation Organization, was, literally, in the scope of the Israel Defense Forces. Arafat was considered by Israel to be an arch-terrorist responsible for killing hundreds of Israelis in Israel and overseas. Nevertheless, then-Defense Minister Ariel Sharon refused to give an "open fire" order. While Sharon's rationale has never been made public, various theories abound including uncertainty regarding the identity of Arafat's successor (in accordance with the timeless principle 'the devil you know is better than the devil you don't know') and operational consequences to the IDF in the context of the War in Lebanon. Be that as it may, it is important for our purposes to note the distinction between the two steps: (1) policy and (2) and its actual "on-the-ground" implementation. While Israel (and Sharon in particular) had defined Arafat as an arch-terrorist when the opportunity presented itself to operationally engage the decision was made to not do so.

Example #2:
In the aftermath of an attack on Israeli athletes and coaches at the 1972 Munich Olympics by the Palestinian terrorist organization, Black September, resulting in the deaths of 11 Israelis, then-Prime Minister Golda Meir ordered the Mossad (the Israeli Security Agency) to kill those responsible in "Operation Wrath of God." Thereafter, Mossad operatives killed those members of Black September involved in planning and executing the attack.[1] The operation was suspended in the aftermath of a tragic instance of mistaken identity when Mossad agents in Lillehammer, Norway, killed an innocent Moroccan waiter, Ahmed Bouchiki, rather than the intended target.[2] While the Israeli public approved of the operation, Meir's decision to suspend the operation in the aftermath of the Norwegian tragedy reflected recognition of the international outrage that followed Bouchiki's killing. In addition, many questions have been asked regarding the operation's legality; the questions focus on whether the operation reflected lawful self-defense or was purely retaliatory in nature. According to media reports those killed were not known to be planning additional acts. If so, the operation would be a violation of international law which does not allow for revenge based State operations. However, according to the then head of the Mossad, Zvi Tsur, the PLO operatives killed in the operation were planning additional attacks against Israel targets. If so, then the operation would conceivably fall under the rubric of anticipatory self-defense (rather than revenge-predicated). Tsur's comments (made in an interview with the Israeli media) have neither been confirmed nor denied by others involved in the operation.

---

[1] For a Hollywood depiction of Meir's decision and its aftermath, see *Black September* by Steven Spielberg.

[2] Ewen MacAskill & Ian Black, *Munich: Mossad Breaks Cover*, THE GUARDIAN, Jan. 26, 2006, http://www.guardian.co.uk/media/2006/jan/26/bbc.israel.

Example #3:

In May 2011, U.S. SEAL forces killed Osama bin Laden in Abottobad, Pakistan. Whether bin Laden was a legitimate target when killed has been subject to some debate;[3] what is unquestioned is that the U.S. government violated Pakistani sovereignty. In that vein, US drone attacks in Afghanistan, Pakistan and Yemen, targeting Taliban and al-Qaeda targets, violate national sovereignty.[4] While the policy reflects President Obama's adoption of President Bush's "National Security Strategy," developed in the aftermath of 9/11,[5] whereby nations hosting terrorists were identified as legitimate targets the measures violate basic sovereignty principles. Whether President Bush intended for purported U.S. allies to be defined as legitimate targets is uncertain; nevertheless, current U.S. policy results in sovereignty violations.

Example #4:

An ill-conceived and poorly planned Mossad operation in Amman, Jordan, resulted in an attempted lethal poisoning, but not killing, of Haled Mashal, a senior Hamas leader. King Hussein, outraged that Israel conducted the attack on Jordanian soil,[6] demanded Israel immediately provide an antidote to Mashal and release the founder of Hamas, Sheikh Ahmed Yassin, from jail. Prime Minister Netanyahu, in the face of unrelenting Jordanian pressure and significant domestic and international criticism of the misbegotten mission, acceded to both of Hussein's demands. The practical consequences were that Mashal survived, Hamas was strengthened, and Israel was embarrassed and therefore weakened. Whether Netanyahu regretted the decision in retrospect is unclear. What is unmistakable is that the operation reflected a stunning disregard of possible consequences from multiple perspectives; foremost among the gratuitous impact on Jordanian-Israeli relations, endangerment of the Israeli public by the forced release of Yassin, and increasing the profile and status of Mashal. Whether the intended death of Mashal outweighed these three significant "costs" is an open question; most experts suggest that the purported benefit of Mashal's death was far outweighed by the foreseeable costs of attempting to kill him.

Example #5:

In October 1995, Mossad agents in Malta killed Fathi Shkaki, the then head of the Palestinian Islamic Jihad. The attack went largely unreported in both the international and Israeli media. In response, carefully placed leaks[7] suggested Shkaki had been killed. Important for our purposes is not the actual attack, rather

---

[3] Sam Jones & Owen Bowcott, *Osama bin Laden's death—killed in a raid or assassinated?*,The Guardian, May 6, 2011, http://www.guardian.co.uk/world/2011/may/06/osama-bin-laden-death-assassination.

[4] http://www.nytimes.com/2012/04/13/world/asia/pakistan-demands-an-end-to-cia-drone-strikes.html?_r=3.

[5] http://georgewbush-whitehouse.archives.gov/nsc/nss/2006/ (last visited Apr. 15, 2012).

[6] Israel and Jordan had signed a Peace Treaty in 1994.

[7] Leaked by Israeli security officials.

what it suggests regarding the importance, from the perspective of state decision makers, of media coverage of operational counterterrorism. The Hebrew adage "if you didn't report it, it didn't occur" is particularly apt in this instance. It is also important to recall that in 1995, the Internet, blogs, and social media were not yet common conveyers of information, and if the mainstream media (print, radio, TV) did not cover a story it went largely unreported. The importance of media coverage cannot be overstated: from the perspective of national decision makers, it sends a powerful message to other terrorist leaders regarding the state's "long arm" and seeks to reassure the public that terrorists "can run but not hide."

Example #6:
According to Israeli intelligence, Sheikh Yassin continued his direct involvement in Hamas operational activities after his release. Yassin had previously been convicted for his role in the abductions and killings of two Israeli soldiers, Avi Sasportas and Ilan Sa'adan, Hamas's initial terrorist attacks. Important to note Yassin was confined to a wheelchair from an early age, and repeatedly insisted he was a religious cleric, not a terrorist. In that vein, Hamas argues it is comprised of two distinct branches: one providing "cradle to grave" social services to the Palestinian population, the other operational (The Izz ad-Din al-Qassam Brigades), conducting terrorist activities against Israeli targets in accordance with the Hamas covenant calling for Israel's destruction. Israel has consistently rejected this distinction arguing Hamas is a terrorist organization, whose members are legitimate targets.[8] Yassin was the subject of two targeted attacks: the first failed,[9] the second succeeded. In the aftermath of the second attack, there was widespread criticism both in the region[10] and internationally. The criticism focused on Yassin's physical condition, highlighting his confinement to a wheelchair, and denied Israel's claim that Yassin was a terrorist rather than a religious cleric. Israeli officials rejected this criticism and claimed that neither his physical ailments nor purported status as cleric granted him immunity from targeted killing particularly because, according to these officials, Yassin was actively engaged in planning and directing terrorist activities.[11]

---

[8] For a broader discussion regarding legitimate targets and Hamas in the context of Operation Cast Lead, see Amos Guiora-David Luban ABA debate; Amos N. Guiora & David J. Luban, *Was the Gaza Campaign Legal?*, ABA NATIONAL SECURITY LAW REPORT, Feb. 2009.

[9] According to unconfirmed reports, the miss was deliberate, intending to send a clear message both that Israel identified Yassin as a legitimate target and that it had successfully penetrated his tight, narrow circle.

[10] Alan Dershowtiz, *Critics of Sheikh Yassin Killing Reveal Own Moral Blindness*, THE JEWISH DAILY FORWARD, Mar. 24, 2006, http://forward.com/articles/6564/critics-of-sheikh-yassin-killing-reveal-own-moral/.

[11] *Id.*

These six examples, then, illustrate the following issues:

Example #	Issue	Target	Outcome	Decision-Maker Factors
1	Considerations beyond the immediate decision to kill a legitimate target	Arafat	Not killed	Uncertainty about successor, operational consequences
2	Sensitivity to criticism in the aftermath of operational error	Munich Olympic attack terrorists	A number of Black September members killed	Cancelled; wrong target killed. Sensitivity to "court of international opinion"
3	Violations of national sovereignty of purported ally	bin Laden	Killed	Violates sovereignty
4	Practical consequences of operational failure	Mashal	Unsuccessful attempt to kill	Failure to consider international relations, endangerment of public, increased profile and status
5	Importance of media reporting	Shkaki	Killed	Lack of media coverage negatively impacts desired effect on terrorists
6	Definition of legitimate target	Yassin	Killed on 2nd attempt	Cleric or terrorist?

These six examples highlight the tension between tactical and strategic decision-making. From a limited tactical perspective, predicated on national security narrowly defined, the intended targets, were uniformly defined as legitimate targets; that said, a caveat must be noted with respect to the legality of Operation Wrath of God if, indeed, intelligence information did not suggest involvement in future terrorist activity. However as the six examples clearly demonstrate, the fact an individual has been identified as a legitimate target does not necessarily mean that a targeted killing will be conducted. After all, as these examples compellingly demonstrate, larger considerations can outweigh otherwise legitimate operational counterterrorism decisions.

These examples illustrate how external factors influence decision-making; simply put, if it were not for significant criticisms, it is safe to assume that Prime Minister Meir would have continued unabated with Operation Wrath of God. It is these "larger" considerations that reflect the multiple tensions inherent to the targeted killing paradigm. With that, we turn our attention back to the 10-point checklist mentioned previously. In doing so, the emphasis is not on the commander's "on the ground" assessment but rather, on considerations that go beyond his area of responsibility and "scope of duty." There is, however, inherent tension in this additional assessment process, primarily because it is the commander who will have direct operational responsibility in the event of a response by the local community. That is, while the commander's assessment regarding a particular targeted killing is essential to the decision-making process, it is not the only consideration in determining whether to conduct a specific action. Conversely it is the commander's responsibility to maintain public order in the area under his operational control.

TEN-POINT CRITERIA-BASED CHECKLIST REVISITED

1. WHAT HAVE BEEN THE LOCAL COMMUNITY REACTIONS TO PREVIOUS TARGETED KILLINGS?

Local communities are generally aware both of whom in their midst is associated with terrorist organizations and to what extent. To that end, given the reality of targeted killings when individuals in leadership positions are killed, the community is not surprised; however, reactions are influenced by collateral damage. With respect to the Obama administration's stated policy, even if the local community is cognizant of the terrorist activities of specific individuals, the argument that those in the midst of a terrorist are *also* legitimate targets has significant "blowback" potential. The decision whether to authorize a targeted killing must include information regarding reactions, both public and private reactions. Important to note that public reactions—demonstrations, civil disobedience, violence—do not necessarily reflect widespread public opinion and may be influenced either by community or external pressures. To that extent, the importance of private reactions cannot be sufficiently emphasized.

2. WHAT HAVE BEEN THE INTERNATIONAL COMMUNITY'S REACTIONS TO PREVIOUS TARGETED KILLINGS?

Needless to say, targeted killings are controversial and subject to significant international concern and criticism. That said, important to distinguish between distinct "noise" levels in seeking to gauge the response level of the international community. For instance, in the immediate aftermath of bin Laden's death, the response in the Arab world was largely muted. While demonstrations took place and threats were issued against the United States, reaction was far less vociferous than one might have imagined. In addition, the reaction of American allies was overwhelmingly positive with the caveat that responses (positive) were necessarily low-key in order to avoid inflaming public sentiment that could have a deleterious impact.

Conversely, in the wake of Anwar al-Awlaki's death, concern was raised primarily among U.S. academics and human rights organizations, regarding the legality of targeting a U.S. citizen.[12] While the response in Yemen was generally muted, as in other Middle East countries, concern raised in the United States led the Obama administration to provide information justifying the attack. While criticism was heard in the United States, the court of international opinion responded very differently. Much as with bin Laden, the response (or lack of) suggested understanding its necessity in the context of aggressive operational counterterrorism. Accordingly, public demonstrations, critical of the action, were largely nonexistent.

That same response held true with respect to the killing of Imad Mughniyah in Damascus. Mughniyah was a senior member of Hezbollah allegedly killed by the Mossad. In the aftermath of his killing, experts predicted Hezbollah would undertake terrorist attacks against Israel. With respect to public response, though some criticism was voiced and a few public demonstrations were held, the general response was muted.

The question, then, is what conclusions can government leaders, planning targeted killings, draw from these examples. Given the volatility of public reaction and its possible impact, decision makers must engage in analysis of predicting community response. As past examples indicate, widespread reaction in the

---

[12] al-Awlaki was the first U.S. citizen to deliberately be killed in a counterterrorism targeted killing operation. Al-Awlwaki is suspected of directing the failed "underwear" bomber, Umar Farouk Abdulmutallab; http://www.washingtonpost.com/world/national-security/al-awlaki-directed-christmas-underwear-bomber-plot-justice-department-memo-says/2012/02/10/gIQArDOt4Q_story.html?wpisrc=nl_headlines.

affected community is largely subdued though certain segments of the greater international community voice criticism.

3. DOES RECENT TERRORIST ACTIVITY/LACK OF TERRORIST ACTIVITY JUSTIFY IMPLEMENTING THE POLICY?

This is a double-edged sword: while a recent terrorist attack may justify an operational counterterrorism response, international law imposes powerful limits on the nation-state. In particular, the state may not engage either in revenge nor retaliation regardless of the severity of the terrorist attack. By example: P. M. Meir's decision to undertake "Operation Wrath of God" was largely understood to be predicated on revenge, therefore violating international law unless intelligence information indicated those targeted were involved in planning additional terrorist attacks. The distinction between revenge and preemptive self-defense cannot be sufficiently emphasized; the former violates international law whereas the latter is justified, subject to principles of morality, necessity, proportionality, and a narrow definition of imminent threat.

In weighing recent terrorist activity or lack of terrorist activity, decision makers invariably draw on the intelligence community in determining both the presumed effectiveness and operational necessity of a potential targeted killing. It is important to recall that a targeted killing is directed at additional audiences, beyond the specific individual. In particular, a successful targeted killing is dependent on penetration of the relevant terrorist cell by the intelligence community. There is a "weak link" in the terrorist organization, and the effort to identify the "mole" is vital. That process is both time consuming and dangerous. It also frequently requires members of the relevant cell to alter their behavior and conduct, including developing new operational methods, identifying new living arrangements, and exposing their families to danger.

If the nation-state has been the target of a series of suicide bombings, there is a greater urgency and justification for heightened sensitivity to future attacks. However, if there has been a significant lull in terrorist activity then, arguably, the weight assigned to future threat may be viewed as less acute. There is neither an empirical approach nor truly inclusive algorithmic model to measure threat; at best, there are assessments and projections predicated on past acts, present circumstances, and indicators regarding future activity. Although operational decision-making necessarily focuses on imminent threats, risks, and dangers, the requirement to take a long-term view largely falls within the bailiwick of national decision makers. To that extent, the decision whether to postpone or cancel when the proposed attack is based on "larger" national calculations rather than specific operational considerations, must be the responsibility of government decision makers. How to respond to either "waves" of suicide bombing or lack of terrorist activity poses significant dilemmas: in the face of the former, the understandable temptation is to operationally engage, whereas the latter, perhaps, creates a paradigm best articulated as a "false sense of security."

4. ARE THERE CURRENT POLITICAL CIRCUMSTANCES THAT PRECLUDE CONDUCTING A TARGETED KILLING?

In determining whether to conduct a targeted killing, it is essential to assess current political developments that may be impacted by a specific operational counterterrorism measure. If, for example, Israeli and Palestinian negotiators are meeting regarding the peace process, the impact of a targeted killing must be carefully weighed. While national security considerations are, naturally, very serious considerations, they are not absolutes.

An additional circumstance that might impact the timing of a targeted killing would be the visit of high-level foreign delegation. While operational circumstances may dictate the timing, it is foreseeable that diplomatic considerations would outweigh immediate national security considerations. That is not to suggest that the latter are not important; rather it is intended to highlight that political and diplomatic factors, situation and circumstance dependent, are sufficiently important to justify postponement of an otherwise legitimate targeted killing.

5. WHAT ARE THE PREDICTED/EXPECTED REACTIONS TO A PROPOSED TARGETED KILLING?

In planning a targeted killing, decision makers must seek to predict possible operational and diplomatic responses. Particularly, the intelligence community must provide assessments regarding the possibility of retaliatory action. In determining the possibility of retaliatory action, the intelligence community must assess a number of factors including the following:

- the capability of a terrorist organization to conduct a retaliatory attack;
- the status of the intended target in the organization and how his anticipated death will impact the organization's operational capability;
- community pressure on the organization to conduct a retaliatory attack;
- earlier responses by the terrorist organization to previous targeted killings (if relevant);
- the identification of targets vulnerable to retaliation (whether domestic or internationally; i.e., embassies, nationals traveling overseas, airlines).

Similarly, the intelligence community, in conjunction with the foreign ministry, must assess the impact of possible international condemnation of a targeted killing. Nevertheless, targeting particular individuals (either status or person specific) may result in diplomatic rebuke. In anticipating possible international response, decision makers must consider "cost-benefit" in assessing the necessity of the attack, or weigh viable alternatives that do not endanger state security. Sensitivity to international criticism reflects geopolitical reality; to what extent it shapes domestic operational counterterrorism policy depends on a variety of factors:

- degree of threat posed by the intended target;
- viability of alternatives;
- impact of diplomatic/international rebuke;
- ability to present compelling counterargument to rebuke;
- possible legal consequences faced by commanders/decision makers with respect to international tribunes or domestic courts in "rebuking" countries;
- ability of state diplomats to "ward off" possible condemnation by sharing, for example, sensitive intelligence information without compromising sensitive intelligence sources.

6. WHAT ARE THE PREDICTED/EXPECTED CONSEQUENCES IF AN OTHERWISE LEGITIMATE TARGETED KILLING IS POSTPONED/NOT CONDUCTED?

This is one of the most difficult questions to properly assess for it requires determining the continued operational capability of a target defined as "legitimate." The individual has been defined by the intelligence community as posing a direct and imminent threat to national security, and in accordance with an aggressive articulation of preemptive self-defense, the individual meets the required criteria necessary to conduct a targeted killing. However, if for a variety of considerations ranging from geopolitical to diplomatic to domestic politics, decision makers determine to postpone an otherwise lawful targeted killing, the impact of *not* conducting the targeted killing must be thoroughly assessed and weighed.

In weighing whether to postpone, decision makers must engage in a sophisticated cost-benefit analysis: the question is whether the threat is so sufficiently imminent that postponement is not a viable option, or whether the threat can be subject to significant mitigation efforts so that the risk incurred by postponement is minimized. Conversely, significant geopolitical developments potentially justify postponement. Whether they justify a decision not to proceed under any circumstances suggests subjecting narrow national security interests to broader national-diplomatic–geopolitical considerations. Doing so suggests the "court of international opinion" outweighs narrowly defined national security concerns. While postponing based on the concerns of the "court of international opinion" is not, inherently, reflective neither of misconstrued policy nor of improper calculations, it is potentially reflective of a "high-risk, low-return" with enormous, negative ramifications if the target defined as legitimate commits a significant terrorist attack.

Given the inevitable finger pointing and recriminations, enhanced by leaks and social media, the political fallout from such a decision (postponement or cancellation) must not be minimized and therefore that "cost" is a factor that absolutely must be taken into consideration.

7. WHAT ARE EXPECTED/PREDICTED GEOPOLITICAL RAMIFICATIONS OF A PARTICULAR KILLING?

In my course "Global Perspectives on Counterterrorism," I emphasize the importance of geopolitical considerations in the context of operational counterterrorism decision-making. In doing so, I suggest to students that the relationship between geopolitics and counterterrorism has historically received insufficient attention from decision makers. Perhaps understandably, national leaders focus on their public in developing, articulating, and implementing counterterrorism policy; after all, their primary obligation is to their public. Targeted killing decision-making reflects specific national security concerns and considerations of a particular nation-state rather than sensitivity to larger international realities.

Nevertheless, given the high profile of targeted killings', failure to incorporate geopolitical considerations in the decision-making process reflects action devoid of a strategic approach to operational counterterrorism. The larger question with respect to the relationship between targeted killing and geopolitics is whether the nation-state views operational counterterrorism through the lens of "unilateralism" or "multi-lateralism". If the former, then geopolitics takes a backseat; if the latter, then geopolitics is essential to the decision-making process.

To wit: President Obama's decision to kill bin Laden had clear impact extending well beyond the location of the "hit" which raised legitimate questions regarding violations of Pakistani sovereignty. From the perspective of the relationship between geopolitics and targeted killing, the bin Laden hit is particularly instructive. While the decision was implemented exclusively by U.S. forces its ramifications extend well beyond Washington and Islamabad: U.S. allies, neither consulted in advance nor participating in its execution, were similarly vulnerable to "response" attacks by al-Qaeda.

Few targets are of the magnitude and significance of bin Laden; nevertheless, analyzing a targeted killing exclusively through the lens of the specific actor (the nation-state) is problematic because particular counterterrorism measures implemented by a nation-state impact other nation-states not involved in the specific attack. The impact on both the international community at large and particular nation-states includes the following:

1. **International developments** (i.e. while the international community is engaged in efforts to convince the Iranian regime to halt its nuclear development project, the impact of an attack on an Iranian scientist or official would be, potentially, enormous as it would be perceived by the international community as a deliberate effort to de-rail the attacks and would be portrayed by Iran as reflective of duplicity and lack of genuine intention to resolve the crisis);
2. **Increasing risk to other nation's assets** (if terrorist organizations identify a non-attacking nation as supportive or complicit in the attack, regardless of the assumptions' veracity);
3. **Condemnation in international forums** (i.e., UN/NGO's requiring expenditure of significant political capital to minimize the fallout of a particular attack. The reference is to American efforts in the UN in response to criticism of Israeli counterterrorism measures);
4. **Impact of accusations of "collusion"** (the reference is to accusations leveled by terrorist organizations against nations including Yemen and Pakistan, in that they are U.S. "stogies" because the United States conducts targeted killing attacks on their soil).

8. DO RECENT LEGISLATIVE OR JUDICIAL DECISIONS IMPACT EXECUTIVE BRANCH DECISION-MAKING WITH RESPECT TO THE TARGETED KILLING POLICY?

Depending on the legal, political, and judicial paradigm in the relevant society, executive branch decision-making may be influenced by robust judicial review and/or legislative action. The most obvious example is the decision by the Israel Supreme Court sitting as the High Court of Justice holding targeted killing, while lawful, must be subject to particular restraints. The Israel Supreme Court addressed the issue in *The Public Committee against Torture in Israel vs. The Government of Israel*. In his seminal decision, President (akin to Chief Justice) Barak wrote the following regarding identification of the legitimate target:

> On the one hand, a civilian taking a direct part in hostilities one single time, or sporadically, who later detaches himself from that activity, is a civilian who, starting from the time he detached himself from that activity, is entitled

> to protection from attack. He is not to be attacked for the hostilities which he committed in the past. On the other hand, a civilian who has joined a terrorist organization which has become his "home," and in the framework of his role in that organization he commits a chain of hostilities, with short periods of rest between them, loses his immunity from attack "for such time" as he is committing the chain of acts. Indeed, regarding such a civilian, the rest between hostilities is nothing other than preparation for the next hostility.[13]

The Court emphasized that not all targeted killings are identical, and that therefore not all targeted killings are authorized by law.[14] I have previously argued that were the U.S. Supreme Court to adopt an approach of active (i.e., aggressive) judicial review not predicated on deference to the executive, many of the Bush administration policies (such as torture, military commissions, indefinite detention) would have been subjected to the strict scrutiny and bright lights they so deserved. Critics of my proposal respond that the American judicial system is different than the Israeli system, making the comparison untenable. Although the systems are indeed different, there are important lessons to learn from the Israeli Supreme Court decision, in particular that the executive branch is not immune from judicial review for deference does not benefit the state or the individual petitioner.

9. WHAT WEIGHT IS ASCRIBED TO SOVEREIGNTY CONSIDERATIONS?

Operational counterterrorism conducted internationally inherently raises questions regarding sovereignty: the most obvious example is the killing of bin Laden on Pakistani soil. While the United States and Pakistan are allies, the relationship is extraordinarily complicated—fraught with dangers, tensions, and risks. According to available information, the decision and implementation was made without consulting or informing Pakistani officials; the reasons for doing so are largely attributable to legitimate U.S. concern that the Pakistani national security infrastructure was complicit with bin Laden and therefore sharing information of the attack would endanger U.S. forces. As evidenced by the fact that bin Laden's compound was in the immediate proximity of a Pakistani military facility, that concern was justified and appropriate. Nevertheless, on the assumption that Pakistani officials were indeed out of the loop, the attack on bin Laden represents a violation of Pakistani sovereignty.

---

[13] HCJ 769/02 The Public Committee Against Torture in Israel v. The Government of Israel [2006], available at http://elyon1.court.gov.il/files_eng/02/690/007/A34/02007690.a34.htm.

[14] *See* http://elyon1.court.gov.il/files_eng/02/690/007/A34/02007690.a34.htm.

As sovereignty is a bedrock principle both of international law and international relations, the question is whether national security of country "A" justifies violating the sovereignty of country "B" when the intended target is terrorist organization, "C." That is, while Pakistan was not the intended target of the hit, the impact on Pakistan is undeniable. Whether perceived as complicit in the attack (and therefore vulnerable to attacks) or weak in the eyes of its own public (and therefore weakened domestically), Pakistani officials are placed in a "lose-lose" paradigm. While U.S. officials may justifiably suggest that Pakistan brought this situation on itself, resulting from its cooperation with bin Laden, the reality is that the United States conducted an attack on an ally's territory. The question then is whether operational counterterrorism justifies violating national sovereignty, reflecting an extraordinarily broad interpretation of aggressive self-defense.

That question takes on increased relevance given media reports that the United States is considering drone attacks against drug cartel leaders in Mexico.[15] In considering such a measure, the United Sates is signaling to Mexican leadership a deep concern regarding the effectiveness of Mexican drug policy while also suggesting that U.S. national security takes precedence over Mexican national sovereignty, even though Mexico is a U.S. ally. This too represents an expanded articulation of self-defense because it equates the threat posed by drug cartels to traditionally understood national security risks.

10. IS DOMESTIC PUBLIC PRESSURE A CONSIDERATION (PARTICULARLY IN THE AFTERMATH OF A TERRORIST ATTACK)?

Politicians are naturally sensitive to public opinion; it is a requirement for holding elected office. In the immediate aftermath of terrorist attacks (particularly when results are acute), the public clamors for something "to be done," though what that exactly means is often an open question. Such a reaction is understandable: innocent individuals have been randomly attacked, the population feels particularly vulnerable, and the media and politicians (not in government) are banging the proverbial war drums. It is at this moment that government responsibility, maturity, and accountability are subject to the greatest scrutiny. It is where the rubber hits the road with respect to counterterrorism. If government leaders had previously developed, articulated, and tested counterterrorism policy, then non-reaction may have been identified as both effective and legitimate.

However, if government leaders failed to engage in the three "P's" (prediction, preparation, and practice) in developing counterterrorism policy, then overreaction

[15] *See* http://www.texasobserver.org/lalinea/congressman-suggests-drone-strikes-in-mexico.

may tragically be all but inevitable. The ramifications of a counterterrorism policy reflecting instinctual response rather than considered and weighed measures are generally and significantly problematic. As history repeatedly demonstrates, panicked responses result in significant violations of individual rights with legitimate questions of whether or not national security is enhanced in the end. Though public opinion may support—if not demand—a powerful reaction, the most effective response may well be silence. Though silence is not popular from the public's perspective, its impact from an operational perspective cannot be overstated.

Overreaction may result in both undesired blowback and international condemnation, whereas under reaction may be perceived by terrorist organizations as weakness in the face of terrorism. In that regard, nonresponse can be effective precisely because the terrorist organization (responsible for the attack) and its community (actively involved) and followers (passive) expect a strong response. A deliberate, thoughtfully considered *lack of response* might have a disquieting effect on members and nonmembers alike. Simply put, they are left guessing as to when the response will occur.

Conversely, a weak and ineffectual response signals to the terrorist organization that while the nation-state has the means to respond, it does not have requisite intelligence information to identify those responsible for the attack. Signaling that weakness is a cost that government must weigh with the utmost gravity; while the lack of intelligence information significantly limits operational choices, a long-term strategic approach to operational counterterrorism as compared to short-term tactical reaction is ultimately more effective. Insufficient intelligence information (which limits operational options) reinforces the centrality of intelligence to the targeted killing paradigm; simply put, devoid of "actionable" intelligence information, the nation-state cannot engage in operational counterterrorism conducted in accordance with the rule of law (public clamor notwithstanding).

7

MORALITY

BY WAY OF a brief preface to this chapter, morality is (and should be) an inherent part of all targeted killings, but there are particular concerns regarding UAV's (unarmed aerial vehicles). When I sent my son was inducted into the IDF, my concerns would have been innumerably accentuated were he the "drone guy," because morality is not sufficiently discussed with respect to the drone policy. There is a sense that I am exaggerating; I do so purposefully because of how extraordinarily relevant this is to the new form of warfare. I truly believe its importance cannot be overstated; in other areas of armed combat, there are clearly established standards of morality that should be similarly developed and applied to robotic warfare. This belief was one of the purposes in undertaking this book project and is the focus of this chapter.

The combination of morality and targeted killing is not a natural fit; it is an awkward and perhaps forced relationship. However, the centrality of morality to targeted killing cannot be sufficiently emphasized. It is not a mantra or cliché intended to soothe understandable criticism, but rather need be a core consideration in every targeting decision. Emphasizing the importance of morality raises legitimate concern whether it complicates the laws of war and accentuates the amorphousness of armed conflict. This concern is understandable and legitimate given both the amorphousness of the term and its uncertain relationship to the act of killing another human being.

FOUR CONCERNS

In researching and writing this book, in particular the issue addressed in this chapter, I have had the opportunity to speak before a wide range of audiences in Israel, the Netherlands, the United Kingdom and the United States. Regardless of how audience members responded to the broad discussion regarding targeted killing, invariably there were strong reactions when the discussion focused on morality. Responses to the suggestion that morality was essential to armed conflict, both in the present and future, were, largely, divided into four distinct camps:

1. Morality and killing are mutually exclusive;
2. Discussing morality endangers soldiers;
3. Targeted killing is illegal; therefore there is no need to discuss morality;
4. International law is sufficient in addressing morality concerns, and introducing morality confuses the situation.

The conversation was spirited and engaging primarily because the proposed nexus between morality and armed conflict arguably complicates the latter, and the former raises profoundly important questions related to values and religion. The dialogue on the relationship between morality and armed conflict was immeasurably more pointed than discussion about the law and armed conflict.

It is as if the law articulates acceptable norms[1] whereas morality represents normative architecture introducing ambiguity and undue burdens to situations that are, according to concerned voices, largely black and white. Casual perusal of contemporary dilemmas confronting soldiers suggests anything but clarity; if anything, armed conflict today, and in all likelihood tomorrow, is enormously cloudy. The lack of clarity is largely a function of the fact that terrorists comingle among the innocent civilian population and that soldiers are hard pressed to distinguish between a legitimate target and a noncombatant. In the traditional war paradigm, soldiers are engaged in combat with each other, whereas terrorism is largely defined by uncertainty—from the soldier's perspective—regarding which individual poses a threat whether to soldier and society alike. That lack of clarity with respect to *who* poses a threat stands in direct contrast to recognition that terrorism (in both practice and theory) poses a threat. Resolving this tension is in many ways the key to a counterterrorism policy based both on the rule of law and morality. While international law imposes requirements on the nation-state regarding use of state power, morality is largely self-imposed subject to self-regulation and internal codes of conduct.

Nevertheless, because counterterrorism cannot rely exclusively on operational measures, how the nation-state conducts itself is of extraordinary importance.

---

[1] Though talkbacks and public discussion suggest this, too, is subject to criticism as it is perceived as a burden imposed on soldiers.

While imposing punitive measures on a terrorist's community, detaining suspected terrorists, and killing individuals deemed to pose an immediate danger to national security is the essence of operational counterterrorism, there is another, distinct, aspect to counterterrorism. Often referred to as "soft" counterterrorism—economic development, building hospitals and schools, and creating infrastructure—this additional form of counterterrorism is no less important, or relevant, than operational measures. Recognizing the importance of soft counterterrorism implies accepting limits of how and when military power can be used by the nation-state.

The limit is not a reflection of means available but of their effectiveness and efficiency. The modern nation-state has unlimited military means available to it. From state-of-the-art fighter jets, to sophisticated and powerful nuclear submarines, to missiles with extraordinary range, the nation-state is undoubtedly far better equipped than any terrorist organization whose arsenal does not pose an existential threat to any country. However, that qualitative and quantitative advantage does not inherently translate to operational success or advantage. In spite of weapons available, commanders acting in accordance with limits imposed by law and morality can apply force only against legitimate targets only in a discriminating manner.

Because of the difficulty in identifying legitimate targets, morality is essential to minimizing collateral damage. That is, in addition to restrictions imposed by the law, it is essential to signal to the civilian population that all reasonable efforts to distinguish between combatant and noncombatant have been emphasized in training exercises and implemented in the field. Because the law does not provide sufficiently clear and concise guidance in conflicts between state and non-state actors morality *must* be an essential aspect of armed conflict. The morality discussion is extraordinarily relevant to addressing the dilemmas described by some as the "fog of war." Failure to both concretely address morality and impose morality requirements on soldiers is akin to a system whereby operational ambiguity, with its problematic consequences, rules the day. The fallout from a lack of clarity regarding the limits of state power is extraordinary: after all, history is replete with tragic examples of soldiers engaged in combat when rules and limits were not clearly articulated and reinforced by their commanders.

Those limits—predicated on law and morality—must be unequivocally enforced. This requirement is particularly important when the target is 9,000 miles away, whose grainy outline on a screen barely looks like a human being. There is enormous danger in distance, both physical and metaphysical: the danger results from the utter lack of contact between the target and the individual charged with operating a joystick, who is mere seconds from killing an individual identified as a legitimate target. While the targeted killing paradigm intends to minimize the loss of life of soldiers whose "on-the-ground" presence will be increasingly lessened, there is also danger in this distance. Simply put: distance contributes to troubling dehumanization othe intended target.

THE JOYSTICK OPERATOR

Given the increasing reliance on robotic warfare where the trigger puller (actually the joystick operator) is divorced from the battlefield introducing morality standards into the decision making process is essential. That is the danger of a drone policy whose parameters and contours are not clearly delineated by political leadership. Delineation requires recognition of the limits of power and the absolute commitment to morality. Implementing these standards requires political leadership articulate criteria, guidelines, and process regarding the goals and limits of drone policy. That imposes the requirement to ensure implementation of the policy *absolutely* incorporate recognition that collateral damage must be minimized. Doing so requires application of international law regarding collateral damage and taking the additional step ensuring combatants understand the consequences of their actions regarding combatants and noncombatants alike. That is the essence of morality in armed conflict; effectiveness of targeted killing requires this additional consideration be integral to the decision-making process.

It requires candidly acknowledging when it occurs rather than ducking behind legal obfuscation and spin masters. Suggesting that collateral damage has not occurred in the context of aggressive operational counterterrorism creates a dangerous environment whereby limits of power are not recognized and a honey trap of "no cost" with respect to the killing of individuals occurs. After all, claiming there is no collateral damage suggests, by logical implication, that all individuals killed in drone attacks were legitimate targets.

A brief segue: collateral damage can include soldiers. In April 2011, two American soldiers were accidently killed by an Air Force Predator drone in Afghanistan.[2] A platoon was accidently labeled—in the heat of the moment—as hostile combatants, or rather, legitimate targets. In that instance, there was a clear breakdown among the numerous actors regarding the decision to give the joystick operator the signal to fire.[3] This tragic incident reinforces the need for training, retraining,

---

[2] David S. Cloud & David Zucchino, Multiple missteps led to drone killing U.S. troops in Afghanistan, *Los Angeles Times*, November 5, 2011, http://articles.latimes.com/2011/nov/05/world/la-fg-drone-attack-20111106.

[3] *Id.*

and criteria-based decision-making. Regardless of how "sleek" drone warfare may seem, if devoid of standards and criteria the consequences will be devastating.

There is naturally great discomfort for many in discussing morality in the context of targeted killing. For some, suggesting that morality and targeted killing are somehow related is offensive because of a profound belief that killing another human being is inherently immoral. That belief, predicated on secular values and religious faith alike, cuts across different vectors. It is, obviously, an opinion that has enormous validity: how can killing and morality be viewed as connected and not antithetical?

SELF-DEFENSE AND MORALITY

Article 51 of the UN Charter articulates the principle of self-defense. However, as discussed elsewhere in this book, the UN Charter refers to self-defense in the context of conflict between nation-states rather than between nation-states and non-state actors. However, that gap must not serve as justification for the state not to have the right to engage in self-defense with respect to non-state actors. To suggest otherwise is to deny the core principles of sovereignty and the state's obligation to protect its civilian population. That said, the question is to what extent and under what circumstances does the nation-state engage in self-defense, and what limits does it impose on itself. Given the centrality of the principle of self-defense to operational counterterrorism, it is incumbent to determine the relationship between morality and killing. Failing to do so leaves the door wide open to armed conflict devoid of moral standards and without self-imposed limits. That is a price that innocent individuals must not, under any condition, be forced to pay.

However, considerations of morality are perceived as imposing undue burdens on soldiers confronting terrorists. Those who forcefully dismiss morality considerations argue a soldier's primary obligation is to kill the enemy and protect himself, his fellow soldiers, and society from harm. According to their argument, requiring a soldier weigh morality before pulling the trigger is akin to guaranteeing his own death. Those who subscribe to this theory impose only one obligation on the commander: ensure the safety of his own soldiers. According to this argument, that is the only consideration of relevance regarding armed conflict.

Others have queried whether undue emphasis on morality comes at the expense of respect for the law, which imposes clear restrictions, whereas morality is nebulous, and thereby provides undue "wiggle room" for soldiers. The question was posed in the following manner: why introduce another set of rules on soldiers when existing law provides sufficient context and defines contours regarding limits of state power? Those holding this position, while respectful of the requirement to introduce considerations of morality, suggest the law is sufficient and imposing additional guidelines muddies the waters. This third group appreciates the importance of morality but suggests that it is insufficiently precise, and its introduction will, unintentionally and ironically, minimize the rule of law.

Truth be told, all four responses are understandable intellectually, emotionally, and practically for they reflect the controversy inherent to the discussion. Favorable public opinion polls regarding U.S. drone policy are understandable, particularly given the risk minimization to U.S. military personnel. Opponents of targeted killing correctly suggest it preferable to detain rather than kill the target. From their perspective, the decision to kill an individual not engaged *at that moment* in an act against the nation-state is inherently illegal and immoral. For those opposed to targeted killing, authorizing the killing of another human being predicated on his *expected future action* or the *future import of his present action* violates legal and moral standards alike.

It is for that reason that suggesting morality be an integral aspect of targeted killing decision making is particularly troubling for those deeply opposed to the policy. From their perspective, it is window dressing to frame targeted killing in a morality paradigm; to do so is to sanitize the act of killing another human being. While this argument is not devoid of relevance, it does miss a key point: targeted killing is a reality, and it will continue to be a reality in the future. The question is how can the decision-making process reflect and incorporate standards of morality whereby criteria are not machine driven but reflect human sensitivity, awareness, and experience. Though hard to do, the more appropriate, relevant, and necessary discussion is how to create a paradigm whereby the decision to kill incorporates standards of morality.

If the nation-state adopts an expansive view of when an individual poses a danger, then the range of possible targets dramatically increases. While perhaps attractive from an operational perspective, the ramifications of expanding the field of legitimate targets are not cost free. Important to recall the legitimate target analysis involves a two-part analysis predicated on an "and" relationship rather than merely an "or" relationship. It is not enough to define an individual as a legitimate target, for it is equally essential to define *when* he poses a threat. In other words, determining when an individual otherwise defined as legitimate target is indeed a legitimate target is critical to implementation of targeted killing.

Precisely because of the dangers inherent to targeted killing it is essential to address morality. Failure to directly confront questions of morality suggests the decision-making process is devoid of criteria essential to ensuring protection of innocent individuals. In October 2011, as previously noted, it was widely reported in the media[4] the CIA claimed noncombatants have not been killed in drone attacks conducted in Pakistan. One need not claim particular expertise nor been involved in operational counterterrorism decision making to have responded incredulously. The claim is possible under one of two conditions: either it was an extraordinary misrepresentation of the truth, or anyone and everyone who had been killed was a legitimate target. The first is disturbing, the second stunning. Whatever the basis, it has been thoroughly refuted. The Bureau of Investigative Journalism, a non-profit organization based in London, has investigated and reported on U.S. drone strikes since 2004. Unsurprisingly, their findings corroborate the former claim of misrepresenting the attacks:[5]

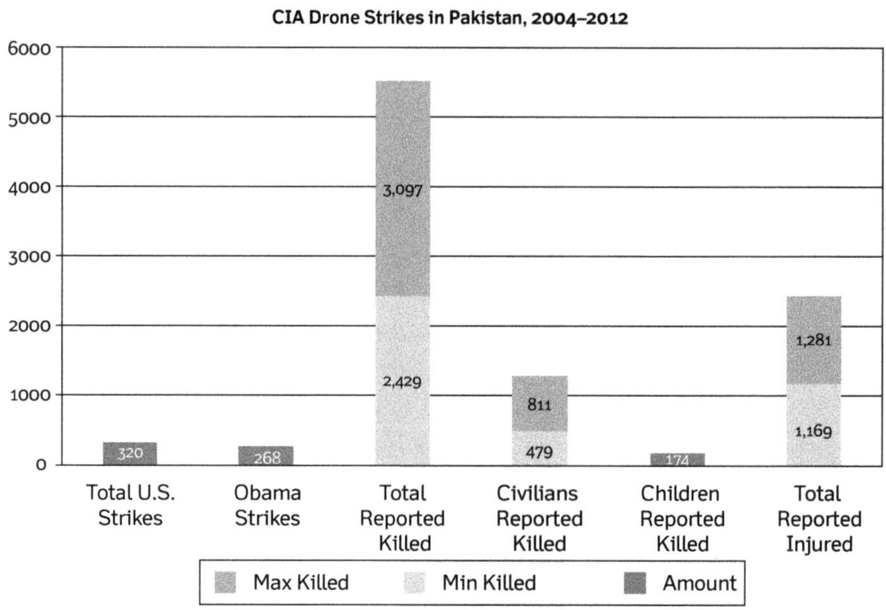

From the perspective of someone whose background is deeply rooted in the legal and policy aspects of operational counterterrorism and had command responsibility for the development of a training video addressing issues of morality in armed conflict, the claim was particularly egregious. It is frankly, all but impossible, to conduct aggressive operational counterterrorism that does not result in some collateral damage. Even international law, which seeks to balance the right of the state to protect itself while imposing the requirement to protect the innocent

---

[4] *See* http://www.nytimes.com/2011/08/12/world/asia/12drones.html?_r=2.

[5] *See* http://www.thebureauinvestigates.com/2012/01/11/obama-2012-strikes/ for the data used in creating this graph.

civilian population, recognizes the reality and inevitability of collateral damage. The burden on the commander requires judicious use of state power; this is particularly the case when the state is engaged in conflict with non-state actors. While engagement is the essence of operational counterterrorism, it must be conducted in accordance with both the rule of law and morality. The CIA claim raises particularly disturbing questions for it suggests the Obama administration is unilaterally redefining legitimate target; the consequences of such a decision are particularly troubling. The troublesome extrapolation from the claim is that an individual in the vicinity of a terrorist is a legitimate target regardless of his (or her) *actual* involvement (whether direct or indirect) in terrorist activity. It is, by analogy, the operational counterterrorism version of "guilt by association" with deeply troubling practical, legal, and moral consequences.

ROBOTIC WARFARE AND MORALITY

In light of these disturbing reports, the requirement to incorporate morality in *all* use of force dilemmas is immeasurably accentuated as the warfare of the future becomes increasingly robotic. Enhanced robotic warfare significantly minimizes human decision making and emphasizes algorithms and mathematical modeling in determining whether an individual is a legitimate target and what conditions justify killing him. The minimization of morality—if not totally ignoring its significance—poses an extraordinarily dangerous "honey trap". Robotic warfare is undoubtedly seductive for it reduces the presence of "boots on the ground," thereby minimizing the direct placement of soldiers in harm's way. Prima facie, that is a legitimate goal;[6] the question, however, is at what cost. It is not a zero-sum game: the decision to minimize loss of a soldier's life by conducting robotic warfare carries a price that must not be ignored. That is not to suggest robotic warfare is inherently unlawful or immoral; the question lies in its implementation and by what criteria and guidelines.

Though tempting and arguably seductive, reliance on robotic warfare is ultimately laden with risks that outweigh perceived benefits. This is particularly the case when the state is targeting specific individuals; essential to this conversation is recognition that at its core, targeted killing reflects a decision by the nation-state to bring its full weight and power on one person's life. This is fundamentally distinct from traditional war conducted in accordance with clear rules, boundaries, and guidelines.

The importance of morality in armed conflict was a central theme to my position as commander of the IDF School of Military Law (SML). In the face of unrelenting

---

[6] I write these lines as the father of a child in harm's way.

criticism by Israeli and international human rights organizations (sometimes justified, sometimes unjustified) regarding conduct of Israeli soldiers at checkpoints in the West Bank, the IDF SML created an interactive video teaching codes of conduct. We did so while working in close cooperation with junior and senior commanders; the decision to make and implement the video directly reflects invaluable cooperation with commanders. If not for their cooperation, the video would be devoid of content and credibility with soldiers, for command influence is essential to both teaching and implementing morality.

There were a number of underlying premises in making the video: morality is "teachable"; morality and international law must and can be taught in a pedagogically engaging and challenging manner; that we need to proactively and creatively address this issue; and command presence and influence is the determining factor in the conduct of a military unit. Notwithstanding much skepticism about the pedagogy of morality, I was and remain convinced that it can, indeed, be taught.

HADITHA

The facts on the ground are distressing: U.S. soldiers killed 24 innocent Iraqi civilians on November 19, 2005, without any apparent cause or justification. Although the number of innocent casualties is not akin to My Lai the actions of the Haditha soldiers is eerily similar. Evidentiary issues may have been the immediate reason for the Haditha plea bargain, but the larger message is troubling on two levels: "How did we get here?" and "How we do go forward?" The answer to both is training, retraining, and additional training, with specific emphasis on morality in armed conflict.

Simply put, Haditha presents a unique teaching moment for the U.S. military. The takeaways are clear: soldiers must be trained intensively, continuously, and repeatedly to distinguish between friend and foe. That is easier said than done, particularly in the amorphousness inherent to a nontraditional war paradigm. Frankly, however, there is no choice but to impose this burden on soldiers regardless of the military circumstances confronting them. Otherwise, justice can never be served either in the zone of combat or in a court of law.

The single most important factor here is the commander. He or she is the linchpin: if a commander discusses rules of engagement and international law obligations while "rolling their eyes," the inevitable misconduct is literally around the corner. I know, for I have seen it. Conversely, a commander who unambiguously demands that his soldiers conduct themselves morally will, in the overwhelming majority of cases, command an operationally effective unit that conducts itself in accordance with the rule of law. The two are not mutually exclusive from an operational perspective.

Quite the opposite: a direct, causal relationship exists between morality in armed conflict, the rule of law and operational effectiveness. That, too, I have seen.

Both issues may have been given lip service in the traditional war paradigm, but their importance is significantly magnified in today's armed conflict scenarios. After all, the zone of combat is ever changing, roving from one village to another, with civilians constantly intermingled with combatants; this poses extraordinary challenges for commanders and soldiers alike. However, that burden cannot and must not be used to justify lax standards and soft criteria in determining whether an individual poses a danger or not.

An approach lacking criteria in determining legitimate targets all but guarantees additional My Lai's and Haditha's. Precisely for that reason, the answer is simple: commanders must directly confront the question of "who is a legitimate target" by imposing narrow definitions. Otherwise, soldiers will, perhaps understandably, take a broad view of "legitimate target" with tomorrow's headlines the inevitable result.

Haditha is thus a powerful reminder that the limits of power predicated on morality and the rule of law must be taught, retaught, and then taught again. Not in a one hour, snap shot, "let's move on" paradigm, but in a consistent, systematic, and systemic manner. Training hours may be limited and subject to innumerable pulls and tugs, but the requirement that morality instruction be at the core of military training cannot be overstated.

This is not simply an internal military or U.S. issue. The anger, frustration, and resentment expressed by Iraqi political leadership in the aftermath of the plea bargain was understandable. No explanation regarding evidentiary weakness and flawed witnesses will convince nor mollify. The perceived reality is that the lives of non-Americans are not valued, and that U.S. military commanders, prosecutors, and judges tolerate killing innocent (fill in the blank regarding which country) citizens. The killing of host nation civilians raises, naturally and understandably, profound questions regarding who the United States perceives as legitimate targets. In other words, who is the enemy? If the enemy is the Taliban and al-Qaeda, then killing subject to rules of engagement is lawful and perhaps welcomed by the local population that has suffered from the presence of both on their soil. However, if the United States is perceived through the lens of the local population as tolerating the deliberate killing of 24 innocent civilians, then probing questions are justifiably posed.

TRAINING FOR THE FUTURE

Failure to address these issues will inevitably raise questions about the true mission of the United States throughout the world. If host nations come to believe the U.S. considers their civilian population as tolerable, if not legitimate, targets, then

U.S. foreign policy is both deeply flawed and profoundly endangered. Teaching morality and ethics during armed conflict to combat units' presents unique challenges to both military educators and commanders.

However, it must be understood from the outset that the ultimate responsibility of morality and ethics is the commander's, in terms of both words and action. If the commander is unwilling to go beyond "talking the talk"; or if his actions contradict what he has instructed his forces regarding issues of morality, the potential for violations by his forces are great. Without internalizing and understanding these concepts, the soldier is being sent into today's battle unprepared. A soldier who goes into battle unprepared is literally a disaster waiting to happen. There are those who argue that a soldier's primary—if not the only task—is the killing of the enemy. The increasing centrality of teaching morality in contemporary armed conflict must be understood. What concerns us is how the contemporary army prepares itself for today's conflict, which is different from yesterday's war. That difference relates to the core question of whom is the soldier fighting: who is the enemy? Contemporary armed conflict does not and will not take place on the vast battlefields of the past; rather, it will occur in the back alleys of Groznyy, Nablus, and Mosul. The soldier will not be facing another soldier wearing a uniform with insignia, carrying his weapon openly, and serving in a unit with a clear chain of command. In the contemporary combat arena, the combat is far more complicated and ambiguous than in traditional warfare for two primary reasons: combat will occur in urban centers and civilians will be present.

The Geneva Convention requires that for a combatant to be designated a soldier, he must wear a uniform with insignia while carrying his weapon openly and be part of a chain of command.[7] Does this mean that the Geneva Convention is irrelevant to contemporary warfare? Not necessarily, but it does suggest that changes may be required in order to ensure continued relevance. What is critical for our purposes is that the Geneva Convention requires an army to educate its forces on issues of international law. In contemporary armed conflict, the soldier placed in the zone of combat (loosely defined as the parameters are ill-defined) will often times encounter an individual wearing civilian clothes—jeans and a tee-shirt are standard attire—without clear certainty as to whether that individual is friend, foe, or perhaps neither. The attire of the foe in contemporary armed conflict is in many ways an effective metaphor for explaining the fundamental change in warfare—from the traditional to the modern. In modern combat, the soldier's world is a much more ambiguous precisely because the combatant standing opposite is at best wearing faded blue jeans, as are all those around him.

---

[7] Geneva Convention (III) Relative to the Treatment of Prisoners of War *opened for signature*, Aug. 12, 1949, art. 4(2).

What complicates the contemporary soldier's mission enormously is that the omnipresent civilians are generally non-participants, meaning they are noncombatants. These civilians are in many cases women and children; what may be said about them, with a fair degree of certainty, is that they are innocent civilians and, therefore, defined as protected individuals according to the Geneva Convention.[8]

A soldier's training is in many ways the teaching of instinctive reactions—better to kill than be killed. "Reaction time is valued," "better to be the initiator," "take the fight to the enemy" are all phrases associated with traditional warfare when the soldier instinctively and clearly knew who was the enemy. The challenge facing commanders is teaching a soldier to respond instinctively and immediately and yet simultaneously determining whether the civilian is a foe, not friend. In a split second that the soldier must distinguish—an international law requirement[9]—between a combatant and the innocent civilian.

If the soldier has been properly trained, not only operationally, but also regarding issues of morality, he will know how to run through a mental checklist absolutely critical to contemporary armed conflict. The civilian—or at least the person dressed like a civilian—may actually be a terrorist; or he may truly be an innocent civilian who desires nothing more than to return home safely to his family. The dilemma facing the soldier who must decide to which population group the individual belongs is literally overwhelming. A wrong decision has potentially dramatic ramifications, not only for those immediately involved in this vignette, but trickle-down effects going far beyond the immediate confrontation.

Teaching morality is difficult; it is amorphous with unclear "curriculum." Nevertheless, it is essential that commanders—senior and junior alike—actively engage training and implementing morality. Failure to do so directly has powerful deleterious consequences from multiple perspectives including operational counterterrorism, unit morale, public perception, and the oft referred to "hearts and minds" of the *other* sides' civilian population. Commanders have increasingly recognized that morality is essential to effective military decision-making; however, that is not enough.

FULL CIRCLE

The extraordinary importance of morality must be clearly articulated to non-military personnel engaged in operational counterterrorism; after all, civilian agencies

[8] Protocol Additional to the Geneva Conventions of Aug. 12, 1949, and Relating to the Protection of Victims of International Armed Conflicts (Protocol I), *opened for signature* June 8, 1977, art. 50.

[9] Protocol Additional to the Geneva Conventions of Aug. 12, 1949, and Relating to the Protection of Victims of International Armed Conflicts (Protocol I), *opened for signature* June 8, 1977, art. 48.

are actively engaged in targeting decisions and their implementation. Under no condition can their civilian status grant them a "deferment" from implementing principles of morality; morality standards must be strictly morality on *all* units and personnel involved in operational counterterrorism. The discussion regarding morality and soldiers is the essence of operational counter-terrorism; its importance cannot be sufficiently emphasized with respect to the interaction between the soldier and the individual standing opposite him. Determining whether that individual is a direct participant is the challenge facing soldiers today. Applying principles of morality, in addition to international law requirements, enhances decision-making that facilitates more effective counter-terrorism.

That requirement takes on a sense of urgency when drone policy increasingly replaces "boots on the ground". When the IDF MSL created the interactive video the audience, message and complexity were clear to all involved. The drone policy as articulated and implemented by the Obama Administration suggests that morality standards are neither articulated nor implemented. That is, frankly, deeply disturbing because U.S. counter-terrorism policy is subject neither to judicial nor legislative review, much less restraint.

President (retired) Barak's theory regarding "self-imposed restraint" takes on greater urgency, then, when the executive branch is unencumbered in applying sophisticated weaponry largely devoid of guidelines and criteria. The essence of morality in armed conflict is particularly acute when the decision to engage an individual is made by a joystick operator thousands of miles removed from the conflict. While the rationale is understandable the danger attendant to the distance coupled with unclear criteria and morality suggests a policy that must be subject to careful review and scrutiny. Operational counterterrorism must have, at all times, one eye firmly focused on the potential tactical target and a second eye, similarly focused, on the larger strategic target. Devoid of clear standards of morality regarding effective engagement with the first target, the second target will be unfocused. The second target is the larger community concerned the nation-state is not sufficiently cautious in defining and identifying a legitimate target; failure to do so both facilitates terrorist organization recruiting and deliberately contributes to future acts of terrorism. In addition, failure to aggressively train and implement morality standards reinforces the notion that the nation-state conducts counter-terrorism indiscriminately reflecting an overly broad articulation of direct participant. Combining morality standards with relevant international law standards, particularly with respect to UAV's, will significantly contribute to a more effective policy steeped in the law and reflecting morality.

8

LOOKING FORWARD

THE PREMISE OF this book is that targeted killing and, in particular, drone policy is here to stay. Opponents, critics, and skeptics may rue this assumption; but frankly speaking, they are wrong. Critics would be better served were they to ask a different question: how can we improve implementation of this new form of warfare? That is the question, and it is the only relevant query that should be posed. I, too, as mentioned throughout this book, am deeply concerned regarding how the policy is articulated and implemented.

My primary concern in this book is to raise a flag—somewhere between yellow and red—regarding a policy that is both "oh so tempting" and "oh so fraught with danger." It is a classic honey trap. Sleek, fast, exciting, new age, high-tech, and "cool." It sounds like Hollywood. Except this is real life with real casualties and real consequences; mistakes, while inherent to operational counterterrorism, must be viewed with extraordinary solemnity both because of their practical consequences and their long-term impact.

Therefore we must ask ourselves what policy makers hope to achieve by the continued implementation of targeted killing, and how/when do they intend to apply this particular method of killing an individual identified as "enemy." These questions are posed in the context of recognition that this is the preferred killing instrument in the years to come. To that end, this chapter will explore both how it will be implemented in the future and the consequences of those decisions.

ISRAEL, HAMAS AND TARGETED KILLING

These lines are written in the immediate aftermath of a targeted killing of Zuhair al-Kaisi by the Israel Defense Forces on March 9, 2012.[1] Al-Kaisi was a leader in the Palestinian Popular Resistance Committee (PRC), the organization responsible for kidnapping Gilad Shalit, and was allegedly (according to the IDF) in the planning stages of an attack on Israel from the Sinai Peninsula.[2] Late last year, al-Kaisi was killed in an air strike. It was rumored that because al-Kaisi's death came six months after the IDF pinned certain killings on al-Kaisi, targeting him was "unfinished business," which if true means that his death was not the result of a lawful targeted killing.

If, however, he was indeed planning additional attacks, detention was operationally unfeasible, and collateral damage had been minimized, then the attack meets the criteria articulated by the Israeli Supreme Court. But there is an additional factor of equal importance: Hamas's response to the attack. In the days following al-Kaisi's killing, Hamas fired rockets into Israel resulting in school closings, business slowdowns and civilians spending significant time in air-raid shelters. In response to those attacks, the IDF conducted aerial raids resulting in the deaths of Palestinian's living in the Gaza Strip. In other words, the targeted killing of al-Kaisi resulted in, or directly contributed to, the continuous cycle of violence that has defined much of the relationship between Hamas and Israel. It is, as one commentator noted, akin to a low-grade fever, with spikes inherent to the malady.

In the context of targeted killing, the question of effectiveness requires a three–part assessment: cost-benefit, prioritization, and resource allocation. All three must be asked in a broader context: did asl-Kaisi present a significant enough intelligence and operational threat that targeted killing was warranted? The question is, obviously, complicated, requiring sophisticated intelligence analysis; after all, it is not enough for the intelligence community to recommend a targeted killing predicated on past acts and a modicum of future activity. Rather, the authorization must be predicated on intelligence information in accordance with the four-part test previously discussed indicative of significant future activity. To engage in a targeted killing when that confluence is not met results in both ineffective operational counterterrorism and, arguably violations of international law.

---

1 Richard Burden, *Why the Sudden Israel—Gaza Escalation?*, THE HUFFINGTION POST, Mar. 11, 2012, http://www.huffingtonpost.co.uk/richard-burden/why-the-sudden-israel-gaza-escalation_b_1337840.html

2 Lilach Shoval, Daniel Siryoti and Shlomo Cesana, *IAF strike kills PRC head who planned attack from Sinai*, ISRAEL HAYOM, MARCH 11, 2012 HTTP://WWW.ISRAELHAYOM.COM/SITE/NEWSLETTER_ARTICLE.PHP?ID=3463.

There are, then, multiple tests and criteria to which a targeted killing decision must be subjected which incorporate questions of law, morality, and effectiveness. The question, in the context of this chapter, is how to apply these three distinct criteria to the future. The responsibility of policy makers is to ascertain that a particular policy is both, at a minimum, effective and legal; with respect to targeted killing, it is essential to incorporate morality considerations precisely because the irreversible consequences of the policy are so powerful and stark.

Subjecting targeting killing to decision-making beyond narrow application of the law is essential to ensuring the policy is not bandied about carelessly or indiscriminately. That is why both considerations of morality *and* rational, criteria-based decision-making reflecting prioritization, risk assessment, and cost-benefit analysis are of paramount importance. It is not enough to identify a target as legitimate; the strategic ramifications of a particular decision are, potentially, sufficiently significant to have profound geopolitical impact extending dramatically beyond the specific "hit." To that extent, the decision whether to engage a specific terrorist in the targeted killing paradigm must not focus exclusively on the individual, regardless of the threat posed. It cannot be sufficiently emphasized how germane additional considerations are in the decision-making process.

IRAN

The question, then, is how does this affect targeted killing policy and decisions going forward? Perhaps the most effective manner to foster the discussion is by focusing on the elephant in the room of geo-political decision-making today. It is to Iran that we turn our attention. Much has been written regarding Iran's efforts to develop a nuclear program; similarly, much has been written regarding international efforts to prevent Iran from succeeding in its efforts.

By way of quick summary: international efforts have primarily focused on diplomatic efforts and economic sanctions. The extent to which these efforts have succeeded is a question of speculation, controversy, and enormous uncertainty; similarly the question of whether military engagement is a viable possibility presents more questions than answers. In that vein, analysts have speculated whether Iranian nuclear sites will be attacked in a manner reminiscent of Israeli attacks on the Iraqi nuclear reactor in 1981 and the Syrian nuclear reactor in 2007.

In 1981, Israeli air force jets successfully attacked Iraq's single nuclear installation; the attack reflected Israel's conviction that Iraq intended to create nuclear weapons to destroy Israel. The Israeli government explained its reasons for the attack in a statement saying: "The atomic bombs which that reactor was capable of producing whether from enriched uranium or from plutonium, would be of the

Hiroshima size. Thus a mortal danger to the people of Israel progressively arose."[3] The attack was widely criticized as an unjustified violation of Iraqi sovereignty; on June 19, 1984, the United Nations Security Council unanimously adopted a resolution "strongly condemning the military attack by Israel as a clear violation of the charter of the United Nations and the norms of international conduct."[4] In 2007, Israeli Air Force jets successfully attacked Syria's nuclear installation.[5] The bombing reflected the Israeli conviction that Syrian nuclear capability posed a direct threat to Israel. Attacking the Iraqi and Syrian reactors was significantly facilitated by the fact that in both cases the reactor was housed in a single facility.

That is in direct contrast to the developing Iranian nuclear program; in a clear example of "lessons learned," Iran has built a number of nuclear sites and dispersed uranium in different locations. Furthermore, the facilities—unlike the Iraqi and Syrian facilities—have been built underground in well-protected bunkers. Over the past few years, the world has increasingly focused its efforts to convince the Iranian regime to stop development of its nuclear program. These efforts have largely, but not exclusively, been based on statements by Iranian leadership regarding the destruction of Israel. Primarily because of the sites' dispersal and their deep entrenchment underground, experts have suggested an attack similar to ones conducted against the Iraqi and Syrian sites is operationally unfeasible. In that vein, experts have suggested that the Iranian program cannot be prevented operationally but can be postponed. That is fundamentally distinct from the Iraqi and Syrian programs; the result of the Israeli attacks was to prevent further development of each country's nuclear project. In the context of postponement, a number of measures have been discussed and implemented ranging from economic sanctions to diplomatic isolation to cyber attacks to physical attacks on Iranian scientists involved in the program's development.

It is to the last measure that we turn our attention: the question is whether targeted attacks against specific Iranian scientists meets the tests of self-defense, morality, and effectiveness proposed in this book. With respect to effectiveness, the critical question is whether the relevant paradigm is prevention or postponement. If the former, it is difficult to assume that the death of one scientist would result in a shutdown of the Iranian nuclear program; if the latter, the answer depends on the particular contribution, involvement, and degree of irreplaceability of the particular scientist. In examining self-defense, the question is whether a nuclear Iran poses a threat and what is the degree and imminence of that threat. Iran's continuously hostile, aggressive and threatening statements regarding Israel

---

[3] http://news.bbc.co.uk/onthisday/hi/dates/stories/june/7/newsid_3014000/3014623

[4] https://litigation-essentials.lexisnexis.com/webcd/app?action=DocumentDisplay

[5] http://www.haaretz.com/news/diplomacy-defense/five-years-on-new-details-emerge-about-israeli-strike-on-syrian-reactor-1.464033.

have convinced Israeli leaders that a nuclear Iran poses a threat to Israeli security; as these lines are written, Prime Minister Netanyahu has consistently articulated that if sanctions and pressures will prove ineffective then operational measures are, from the perspective of self-defense, legitimate.

It is in that context that attacking specific scientists must be analyzed: if intelligence information clearly indicates a particular scientist has a significant role in the program's development, then given threats articulated by the regime, principles of self-defense would suggest a person-specific attack is legitimate. The caveat is whether alternatives (i.e., arrest) are available and the reliability of the available intelligence information regarding the specific involvement of the particular scientist. Regarding morality, the question is whether implementation of a person-specific policy ensures collateral damage is an essential aspect of the decision-making process, and its strategic consequences are carefully weighed. Furthermore, morality considerations impose on decision makers the requirement to determine whether a specific targeted killing is, indeed, essential to the postponement paradigm. Otherwise, the policy will be implemented devoid of standards, guidelines, and criteria.

The discussion regarding Iran is particularly relevant for it cuts to the heart of targeted killing for it focuses on threats, sovereignty, self-defense, and preemption. The question, regarding both targeted killing and the Iranian nuclear reactor is twofold: whether the policy is intended to eradicate or minimize and whether targets will be broadly or narrowly defined. The question, however, is more complicated than that for attacking Iranian officials or scientists can be considered an act of war, unlike the killing of individuals suspected of involvement in terrorism.

The point of departure is whether targeted killing is applicable to state actors or individuals acting on behalf of a state or whose actions benefit a particular nation-state. As evidenced by the killing of specific individuals involved in development of the Iranian nuclear program, nation-states have demonstrated a willingness to apply to the state-state arena a measure generally associated with operational counterterrorism. While the two paradigms—operational counterterrorism and state conflict—are fundamentally different, a similar operational measure is applied to the Iranian nuclear program.

While national leaders and the public alike may wish for both (terrorism and Iran's nascent nuclear project) to simply disappear, reality and history suggest otherwise. With respect to terrorism, nation states can hope to minimize or manage terrorism but to articulate a policy of "defeating terrorism" is fool's gold. With respect to Iran, while experts may point to the eradication of Iraq and Syria's nuclear plants as applicable to Iran, the analogy is an illusion given how Iran has dispersed its sites throughout the country.

Given the operational complexity posed, then, by multiple sites rather than a single facility, the operative question becomes what is the most effective mechanism for impacting the process with the understanding that eradication is, largely, unachievable. What targets are of particular importance, whereby striking them would have both tactical and strategic importance regarding the Iranian plan? This question assumes that widespread targeting is operationally unfeasible, both with respect to expected gains and probable losses. Careful cost-benefit analysis, predicated on the right to engage in preemptive self-defense tempered by operational limitations and sophisticated effectiveness analysis, leads to the conclusion that targeting specific individuals meets criteria proposed throughout this book.

Re-articulated, the criteria-based approach when properly articulated, developed, and implemented, reflects effective balancing of national security considerations and individual rights. In the targeted killing paradigm it imposes, on the one hand, limitations on state power while, on the other hand, enabling application of state power. This balanced approach is predicated on a narrow definition of legitimate target with the specific intent of minimizing collateral damage while engaged in aggressive operational counterterrorism predicated on self-defense principles.

RULE OF LAW AND MORALITY

Essential to a rule of law paradigm is application of a narrow definition of self-defense and broad definition of morality. There is an undeniable tension in this recommendation that implies significant restrictions on the use of state power. It is not, however, to suggest that state power is illegitimate and must not be brought to the fore. Not in the least. It is, nevertheless, intended to create a paradigm in which the use of targeted killing is limited in accordance with the rule of law, morality, and carefully constructed and rigorously applied guidelines.

In that vein, the U.S. drone policy as initially articulated by President Bush and subsequently embraced by President Obama raises powerful questions regarding the confluence of law, morality, and policy. While President Bush's terminology was unfortunate ("dead or alive"), President Obama's policy is not reflective of narrow application of extraordinary state power. In many ways, Obama's policy suggests adoption of Bush's phraseology: a dangerous application of a standard (using the term loosely) whereby the definition of legitimate targets incorporates those in the milieu of suspected terrorists because their innocent civilian status is too hard to verify. That "standard" is suggestive of illegality and immorality.

In the same vein that not all terrorists can be killed, and not all Iranian nuclear sites can be effectively targeted, the operational implementation of a narrow criteria-based approach explicitly suggests person-specific targeting is the essence of lawful and moral use of state power. Targeting broadly is, of course, an intellectual and practical misnomer; person-specific targeting, as compared to nonspecific application of state power, requires careful analysis of numerous factors including degree of threat posed, risk of not responding to a threat (based on intelligence information), and the expected cost (to the civilian population) in the aftermath of an attack.

As suggested in previous chapters, resolution of these dilemmas is complicated and complex. Without doubt, the dilemma of the decision maker in the context of operational counterterrorism and in the face of a nascent nuclear threat requires making difficult choices, often choosing between two, almost equal bad options. That, however, does not justify engaging in a paradigm whereby the definition of collateral damage is dramatically narrowed and the definition of legitimate target is enormously broadened.

By analogy, effective response to the Iranian nuclear threat requires recognition of limited operational choices and the need to engage in narrow implementation of state power. With all the danger inherent to prediction, a large-scale military effort does not seem operationally feasible or likely. Rather, what appears to be the more likely course of action is strategic targeting predicated on person-specific threat analysis; in other words, the manifestation of targeted killing subject to strict scrutiny. In predicting the latter, rather than the former, the working assumption is that preventing Iran from developing a nuclear reactor program is less likely than its postponement.

In many ways, this dilemma—prevention or postponement—is at the core of a larger debate: what is the true purpose and intent of targeted killing? In developing a counterterrorism policy, the nation-state must articulate, and subsequently implement, a specific goal. While defeating terrorism is a worthy aspirational motive, it is, largely, an unreasonable expectation. The more realistic operational goal is to minimize terrorism, perhaps to manage both its costs and impacts. For that very reason, targeted killing rather than a full-scale military operation in the face of terrorism represents decision-making rooted in operational reality.

By analogy, then, a person-specific policy regarding Iran's nascent program represents recognition that postponement (i.e., delay) is more realistic than total prevention. This limited approach reflects the nation-state's right to engage in self-defense based on the over-arching principle of limited use of state power. Conversely, a policy not rooted in this principle would result in wider attacks on broader targets significantly enhancing collateral damage while raising legitimate questions regarding effectiveness, legality, morality, and operational intent. Targeted killing as proposed in this book represents a limited measure in the face of a known and identified threat; at its core, the policy reflects limited use of state power specifically targeting a particular individual subject to rigorous standards of necessity. In other words, the need to minimize collateral damage is an absolute. To ensure this test is robustly applied requires decision makers recognize the obligation to distinguish legitimate targets from noncombatants is essential. That requirement cannot be negated by reliance on legal nuance reflecting the "square peg in a round hole" paradigm.

TARGETED KILLING AND SELF-DEFENSE

The question is the implementation of self-defense: a nation-state that conducts self-defense measures in accordance with Article 51 of the UN Charter will not act preemptively. However, self-defense as practiced by nation-states is largely predicted on preemptive measures that extend beyond the narrow definition and terminology of Article 51. That is, rather than conducting self-defense in full accordance with the UN Charter, nation states choose to act preemptively rather than choosing to respond to an attack that could, possibly, have been thwarted.

As international law makes clear, a critical factor in analyzing the action's legality is ascertaining its proportionality. To that extent, targeting an individual whose role is essential to development of the Iranian nuclear program would, under certain conditions, meet the proportionality requirement. However, assessing the action's legality also requires inquiring whether collateral damage was minimized in accordance with international law requirements. However, even if proportionality and collateral damage requirements are respected, preemptive self-defense is, nevertheless, controversial and subject to criticism and concern. For that very reason it is essential that the policy be applied in a limited manner, subject to powerful self-imposed restraints with a narrow articulation of legitimate target. While self-imposed restraints will, in all probability, neither mitigate nor mollify critics, it represents a balanced approach predicated on the policy's continued implementation.

Similarly, the drone attack that killed Anwar al-Awlaki also raises significant questions of policy implementation focusing, in large part, on two issues: the targeted killing of American citizens, and the possible violation of state sovereignty. The administration justified the killing in the following manner:

> The legal analysis, in essence, concluded that Mr. Awlaki could be legally killed, if it was not feasible to capture him, because intelligence agencies said he was taking part in the war between the United States and Al Qaeda and posed a significant threat to Americans, as well as because Yemeni authorities were unable or unwilling to stop him.[6]

---

[6] http://www.nytimes.com/2011/10/09/world/middleeast/secret-us-memo-mad

On March 5, 2012, Attorney General Holder addressed the al-Awlaki killing; in justifying the attack, Holder said that the president has the ability—through the Constitution—to order the death of citizens abroad if they are believed to pose an imminent threat to the United States.[7] While there is widespread consensus regarding al-Awalki's past actions, the question in the targeted killing paradigm, subject to international law and morality standards, is whether reliable intelligence information was indicative of his involvement in future terrorist activity. That is, was al-Awlaki killed as "payback" for past acts, or was the action truly intended to prevent future actions?

Much of the discussion has focused on the legality of killing an American citizen deprived of recourse to judicial process. While I am of the opinion that if an American citizen (outside the United States) is actively engaged in terrorist activity, and his detention is operationally not feasible, then a targeted killing is justified subject to the caveats discussed in this book. However, the legality of the act depends on implementation of standards, criteria and guidelines; in other words, payback—regardless of citizenship—violates international law and morality alike. In the context of "looking forward," the question is not the citizenship of the intended target (status) but is exclusively dependent on his/her involvement in future acts of terrorism (conduct).

As to Iran: whether future targets include individuals with specific responsibility for the nuclear program's continued development is an open question. It is, I propose, both a valid application of targeted killing and preferable from an operational perspective to full military engagement fraught with extraordinary unknowns. In a targeted killing paradigm predicated on the rule of law and sophisticated effectiveness assessment, the burden on the state is to strictly define a legitimate target. If the operational decision regarding Iran's nuclear program is to endeavor to postpone, rather than prevent, then targeted killing provides decision makers with an immensely effective tool.

The question, obviously, is identifying legitimate targets. Akin to the suicide bomber infrastructure, there are multiple actors whose contribution to the program is sufficiently important to classify them as legitimate targets. Important to add: legitimacy of targeted killing is dependent on narrow classification rather than broad, indiscriminate classification. In other words, specific targeting of individuals whose actions significantly endanger national security. The test, to meet rule of law and morality standards, must be rigorously applied; as history has demonstrated responses not reflecting that rigor inevitably contribute to significant violations of individual rights. The results of such panic responses are

---

[7] http://www.salon.com/2012/03/06/attorney_general_holder_defends_execution

clear: widespread collateral damage significantly enhancing the risk of "blowback." In other words, a targeted killing policy not deeply rooted in the rule of law and morality is, ultimately, an ineffective operational measure.

FINAL WORD

To that end, it is incumbent upon decision makers—particularly in implementing a policy predicated on Hollywood-like operational measures—to ensure that decisions reflect carefully articulated and narrowly applied criteria and standards regarding a legitimate target. As mentioned in the preface, the impetus for this book is my experience in the legal and policy aspects of operational counterterrorism. To that end, I approach the questions posed in this book from the perspective of having had a seat at the table; the concerns raised in the preceding pages reflect my concern regarding the use of state power. While I fully support and understand the state's right to engage in aggressive self-defense, the question is one of degree and standards. Perhaps more than anything else, it is my deep concern that criteria regarding legitimate target and threat have not been fully and consistently articulated and implemented. In the context of targeted killing, the danger of failing to narrowly define both terms directly leads to violations of the rule of law and morality. Given the lure of high-tech warfare my concern is deep; that concern has convinced me that application of the rule of law and morality standards take on heightened urgency.

Index

www.ingramcontent.com/pod-product-compliance
Ingram Content Group UK Ltd.
Pitfield, Milton Keynes, MK11 3LW, UK
UKHW021133160926
475595UK00020B/31

9 780199 969739